INSPIRING
EXPERIENCES
THAT
BUILD FAITH

INSPIRING EXPERIENCES THAT BUILD FAITH

FROM THE LIFE AND MINISTRY OF

THOMAS S. MONSON

Deseret Book Company
Salt Lake City, Utah

Library of Congress Cataloging-in-Publication Data
Monson, Thomas S., 1927–
    Inspiring experiences that build faith / Thomas S. Monson.
        p. cm.
    Includes index.
    ISBN 0-87579-901-9
    1. Monson, Thomas S., 1927– . 2. Church of Jesus Christ of
Latter-day Saints—Clergy—Biography. 3. Mormon Church—Clergy—
Biography. 4. Christian life—Mormon authors. I. Title.
BX8695.M56A3   1994
289.3'32'092—dc20   94–28433
[B]   CIP

Printed in the United States of America
10   9   8   7   6   5   4   3   2

CONTENTS

֍

Service to Others

Contents

Faith Precedes Blessings

Contents

Prayer Availeth Much

Missionary Moments

Contents

Contents

Testimony Teaches Truth

Example of the Believers

Contents

On the Lighter Side

SERVICE TO OTHERS

When ye are in the service
of your fellow beings
ye are only in the service
of your God.

MOSIAH 2:17

A Lesson in Reverence

&

When I was a boy in Primary, one day as we left the chapel for our classrooms I noted that our Primary president, Melissa Georgell, remained behind, sitting alone on the front row of benches. I paused and observed her and saw that she was weeping. I walked up to her and said, "Sister Georgell, why are you crying?"

She wiped her eyes with her lace handkerchief and said, "I feel that I'm a failure as a Primary president. I can't control the Trail Builders. Could you help me, Tommy?"

I promised her that I would. What I didn't know then is that I was the source of her tears. She had effectively enlisted me to aid in achieving reverence in our Primary. And we did achieve it.

The years flew by. Melissa, now in her nineties, lived in a nursing facility in the northwest part of Salt Lake City. Just before Christmas I determined to visit my beloved Primary president. Over the car radio, I heard the song "Hark! the herald angels sing; Glory to the newborn King!" I reflected on the visit made by wise men those long years ago. They brought gifts of gold, of frankincense, and of myrrh. I brought only the gift of love and a desire to say thank you.

I found her in the lunchroom. She was staring at her plate of food, teasing it with the fork she held in her aged hand. Not a bite did she eat. As I spoke to her, my words were met by a benign but blank stare. I gently took her fork and began to feed her, talking all the time I did so about her service to boys and girls as a Primary worker and the joy that was mine to have served later as her bishop. There wasn't so much as a glimmer of recognition, far less a spoken word. Two other residents of the nursing home gazed at me with puzzled expressions. At last they spoke, saying, "She doesn't know anyone—even her own family. She hasn't said a word for a long, long time."

Lunch ended. My one-sided conversation wound down. I stood to leave. I held her frail hand in mine and gazed into her wrinkled but beautiful countenance. "God bless you, Melissa," I said, "and merry Christmas."

Without warning, she spoke the words, "I know you. You're Tommy Monson, my Primary boy. How I love you."

She pressed my hand to her lips and bestowed on it the kiss of love. Tears coursed down her cheeks and bathed our clasped hands. Those hands, that day, were hallowed by heaven and graced by God. The herald angels did sing, for I heard them in my heart.

A Christmas Train

One ever remembers that Christmas day when giving replaces getting. In my life, this took place in about my tenth year. As Christmas approached, I yearned as only a boy can yearn for an electric train. My desire was not to receive the economical and everywhere-to-be-found windup model train; rather, I wanted one that operated through the miracle of electricity. The times were those of economic depression; yet Mother and Dad, through some sacrifice, I am sure, presented to me on Christmas morning a beautiful electric train.

For hours I operated the transformer, watching the engine first pull its cars forward, then push them backward around the track. Mother entered the living room and told me that she had purchased a windup train for Mrs. Hansen's son Mark, who lived down the lane. I asked if I could see the train. The engine was short and blocky, not long and sleek like the more expensive model I had received. However, I did take notice of an oil tanker car that was part of his inexpensive set. My train had no such car, and pangs of envy began to be felt. I put up such a fuss that Mother succumbed to my pleadings and handed me the oil tanker car. She said, "If you need it more than Mark, you take it." I put it with my train set and felt pleased with the result.

Mother and I took the remaining cars and the engine down to Mark Hansen. The young boy was a year or two older than I. He had never anticipated such a gift and was thrilled beyond words. He wound the key in his engine, it not being electric like mine, and was overjoyed as the engine and two cars, plus a caboose, went around the track. Mother wisely asked, "What do you think of Mark's train, Tommy?"

I felt a keen sense of guilt and became very much aware of my selfishness. I said to Mother, "Wait just a moment. I'll be right back!"

As swiftly as my legs could carry me, I ran to our home, picked up the oil tanker car, plus an additional car from my train set, and ran back down the lane to the Hansen home, and joyfully said to Mark, "We forgot to bring two cars that belong to your train." Mark coupled the two extra cars to his set. I watched the engine make its labored way around the track and felt a supreme joy, difficult to describe and impossible to forget. The spirit of Christmas had filled my very soul.

Two Pet Rabbits

When I was about eleven and holiday time had come, we were preparing for the oven a gigantic turkey and anticipating the savory feast that awaited. I was playing with a neighborhood pal of mine in my yard when he made the observation, "It sure smells good in your house. What are you having for dinner?" I told him we would be having a turkey dinner. He then asked a question that was startling to me: "What does turkey taste like?"

I responded, "Oh, about like chicken tastes."

Again a question: "What does chicken taste like?"

It was then that I realized my friend had never eaten chicken or turkey. I asked what his family was going to have for their holiday dinner. There was no prompt response—just a downcast glance and the comment, "I dunno. There's nothing in the house."

I pondered a solution. There was none. I had no turkeys, no chickens, no money. Then I remembered I did have two pet rabbits. They were the pride of my life, two beautiful New Zealand whites. I said to my friend, "You come with me, because I've got something for your dinner." We went to the rabbit hutch, and I opened it, placed the two rabbits in a box, and said, "You take these home, and your dad will know what to do with them. They taste a whole lot like chicken."

He took the box, climbed the fence, and headed for home, a holiday dinner safely assured. Tears came easily to me as I closed the door to the empty rabbit hutch. But I was not sad. A warmth, a feeling of indescribable joy, filled my heart. My friend later said that had been the best holiday dinner they had ever had.

Uncle Elias

Seemingly little lessons of love are learned by children as they silently observe the examples of their parents. My own father, a printer, worked long and hard practically every day of his life. I'm certain that on the Sabbath he would have enjoyed just being at home. Rather, he visited elderly family members and brought cheer into their lives.

One such family member was his uncle, who was crippled by arthritis so severe that he could not walk or care for himself. On a Sunday afternoon Dad would say to me, "Come along, Tommy. Let's take Uncle Elias for a short drive." Boarding the old 1928 Oldsmobile, we would proceed to Eighth West, where, at the home of Uncle Elias, I would wait in the car while Dad went inside. Soon he would emerge from the house, carrying in his arms like a china doll his frail and crippled uncle. I would then open the door and watch how tenderly and with such affection my father would place Uncle Elias in the front seat so that he would have a fine view while I occupied the rear seat.

The drive was brief and the conversation limited, but oh, what a legacy of love! Father never read to me from the Bible about the good Samaritan. Rather, he took me with him and Uncle Elias in that old 1928 Oldsmobile and provided a living example I have always remembered.

A Wise Adviser and a One-Eyed Pigeon

As a boy of fifteen, I served as president of the teachers quorum of my ward. Our adviser, Harold, was interested in us, and we knew it. One day he said to me, "Tom, you enjoy raising pigeons, don't you?"

I responded with a warm "Yes."

Then he proffered, "How would you like me to give you a pair of purebred Birmingham Roller pigeons?"

This time I answered, "Yes, sir!" The pigeons I had were just the common variety trapped on the roof of the Grant Elementary School.

He invited me to come to his home the next evening. The next day was one of the longest in my young life. I was awaiting my adviser's return from work an hour before he arrived. He took me to his loft, which was in a small barn at the rear of his yard. As I looked at the most beautiful pigeons I had yet seen, he said, "Select any male, and I will give you a female that is different from any other pigeon in the world." I made my selection. He then placed in my hand a tiny hen. I asked what made her so different. He responded, "Look carefully, and you'll notice that she has but one eye." Sure enough, one eye was missing, a cat having done the damage. "Take them home to your loft," he counseled. "Keep them in for about ten days and then turn them out to see if they will remain at your place."

I followed his instructions. Ten days later, upon my releasing them, the male pigeon strutted about the roof of the loft, then returned inside to eat. But the one-eyed female was gone in an instant. I called Harold and asked, "Did that one-eyed pigeon return to your loft?"

9

"Come on over," he said, "and we'll have a look."

As we walked from his kitchen door to the loft, my adviser commented, "Tom, you are the president of the teachers quorum. What are you going to do to activate Bob?"

I answered, "I'll have him at quorum meeting this week."

Then he reached up to a special nest and handed to me the one-eyed pigeon. "Keep her for a few days and try again." This I did, and once more, upon being released, she disappeared. Again the experience, "Come on over and we'll see if she returned here." Came the comment as we walked to the loft, "Congratulations on getting Bob to priesthood meeting. Now what are you and Bob going to do to activate Bill?"

"We'll have him there this week," I volunteered.

This experience was repeated over and over again. I was a grown man before I fully realized that, indeed, Harold, my adviser, had given me a special pigeon, the only bird in his loft he knew would return every time she was released. It was his inspired way of having an ideal personal priesthood interview with the teachers quorum president every two weeks. Because of those interviews and that old one-eyed pigeon, every boy in that teachers quorum became active. I shall always thank the Lord for my quorum adviser and his ability to reach and inspire the president of an Aaronic Priesthood quorum.

Old Bob

I have many memories of my boyhood days. Anticipating Sunday dinner was one of them. Just as we children hovered at our so-called starvation level and sat anxiously at the table with the aroma of roast beef filling the room, Mother would say to me, "Tommy, before we eat, take this plate I've prepared down the street to Old Bob, and then hurry back."

I could never understand why we couldn't first eat and later deliver his plate of food. I never questioned aloud but would run down to his house and then wait anxiously as Bob's aged feet brought him eventually to the door. Then I would hand him the plate of food. He would present to me the clean plate from the previous Sunday and offer me a dime as pay for my services. My answer was always the same: "I can't accept the money. My mother would tan my hide." He would then run his wrinkled hand through my blond hair and say, "My boy, you have a wonderful mother. Tell her thank you."

You know, I think I never did tell her. I sort of felt Mother didn't need to be told. She seemed to sense his gratitude. I remember too that Sunday dinner always seemed to taste a bit better after I had returned from my errand.

Old Bob came into our lives in an interesting way. He was a widower in his eighties when the house in which he was living was to be demolished. I heard him tell my grandfather his plight as the three of us sat on Grandfather's old front porch swing. With a plaintive voice, he said to Grandfather, "Mr. Condie, I don't know what to do. I have no family. I have no place to go. I have no money." I wondered how Grandfather would answer. Slowly Grandfather reached into his pocket and took from it that old leather purse from which, in response to my hounding, he had produced many a penny or nickel for a special treat. This time he removed a key and handed it to Old Bob. Tenderly he said, "Bob, here is the key to that house I own next door. Take it. Move your things in there and stay as long as you like. There will be no rent to pay and nobody will ever put you out again."

Tears welled up in the eyes of Old Bob, coursed down his cheeks, then disappeared in his long, white beard. Grandfather's eyes were also moist. I spoke no word, but that day my grandfather stood ten feet tall. I was proud to bear his given name. Though I was but a boy, I learned a great lesson on love that day.

The True Shepherd

&

As I was growing up, our family, in the springtime and in the fall, would drive to Provo Canyon. We boys were always anxious to get on the fishing stream or into the swimming hole, and we would try to push the car a little faster. In those days, my father drove an old 1928 Oldsmobile, and if he went over 35 miles an hour, my mother would say, "Keep it down! Keep it down!" I would say, "Put the accelerator down, Dad! Put it down!"

Dad would stay at about thirty-five miles an hour all the way to Provo Canyon, until we would at times come around a bend in the road and run straight into a herd of sheep. We would come to a standstill as hundreds of sheep would file past us, seemingly without a shepherd, a few dogs yapping at their heels as they moved along. Way in the rear we could see the horse—with not a bridle on it, but a halter—and the sheepherder. He was occasionally slouched down in the saddle dozing, as the horse knew which way to go, and the yapping dogs did the work.

Contrast that to the scene I viewed years later in Munich, Germany. It was a Sunday morning, and we were en route to a missionary conference. As I looked out the window of the mission president's automobile, I saw a shepherd with a staff in his hand, leading the sheep. They followed him wherever he went. If he moved to the left, they followed him to the left. If he moved to the right, they followed him in that direction.

I made the comparison between the true shepherd and the herder with his yapping dogs. Jesus is our exemplar. He said, "I am the good shepherd, and know my sheep." (John 10:14.)

A Grateful Student

One day I saw a grown man cry. It wasn't his custom. The tears stemmed not from sorrow but from gratitude. My swimming coach, Charlie Welch, who perhaps aided more boys than did any other man to achieve their swimming skills and successfully earn their Life Saving Merit Badge, was calling the roll of our swimming class at the University of Utah. His voice resounded from the plaster walls. The gym door opened that day in 1944, during World War II, and there entered a young man in Navy uniform. The sailor came up to Charlie and said, "Excuse me, but I want to thank you for saving my life."

Charlie lifted his eyes from the roll card, put the pencil in his pocket, and asked, "What's that?"

Again the sailor said, "I want to thank you for saving my life. You once told me that I swam like a lead ball, yet you patiently taught me to swim. Two months ago, far off in the Pacific, an enemy torpedo sank my destroyer. As I swam my way through the murky waters and foul-tasting, dangerous film of oil, I found myself promising, 'If I ever get out of this mess alive, I'm going to thank Charlie Welch for teaching me, as a Boy Scout, how to swim.' Today I came here to say thank you."

Twenty athletes stood shoulder to shoulder and never uttered a word. We watched the great tears of gratitude well up in Charlie's eyes, roll down his cheeks, and tumble upon his familiar gray sweatshirt. Charlie Welch, a humble, prayerful, patient, and loving builder of boys, had just received his reward.

Determined Magazine Representatives

&

When I was bishop of the Sixth-Seventh Ward in Salt Lake City, I noted that our record for subscriptions to the *Relief Society Magazine* was low. Prayerfully my counselors and I analyzed the names of the individuals whom we could call to be magazine representative. The inspiration dictated that Elizabeth Keachie should be given the assignment. I approached her with the task, and she responded, "Bishop Monson, I'll do it."

Elizabeth Keachie was from Scotland, and when she replied, "I'll do it," one knew she indeed would. She and her sister-in-law, Helen Ivory, commenced to canvass the ward, house by house, street by street, and block by block. The result was phenomenal. We had more subscriptions to the *Relief Society Magazine* than had been recorded by all the other units of the stake combined.

I congratulated Elizabeth Keachie one Sunday evening and said to her, "Your task is done."

She replied, "Not yet, Bishop. There are two blocks I have not yet covered."

When she told me which blocks they were, I said, "Sister Keachie, no one lives on those blocks. That area is all industrial."

"Just the same," she said, "I'll feel better if I go and check them myself."

Sister Keachie and her companion, on a rainy day, covered those final two blocks. On the first one, she found no home, nor did she on the second. She and Sister Ivory paused, however, at a driveway that was strewn with mud from a recent storm. Sister Keachie gazed down the driveway perhaps a hundred feet and there noticed a garage. This was not a normal garage, however, in that there was a curtain at the window.

She turned to her companion and said, "Sister Ivory, shall we go and investigate?"

The two sweet sisters then walked through the mud for forty feet to a point where the entire garage could be seen. Now they noticed a door that had been cut into the side of the garage, which door was unseen from the street. They also noticed that there was a chimney with smoke rising from it.

Elizabeth Keachie knocked at the door. A man of about sixty-five years of age, William Ringwood, answered. They then presented their story concerning the need of every home having the *Relief Society Magazine*. William Ringwood replied, "You'd better ask my father." Ninety-three-year-old Charles W. Ringwood then came to the door and also listened to the message. He subscribed.

Elizabeth Keachie reported to me the presence of these two men in our ward. When I requested their membership certificates, I received a call from the Membership Department at the Presiding Bishopric's Office. The clerk said, "Are you sure you have living in your ward Charles W. Ringwood?"

I replied that I was sure, whereupon the clerk reported that the membership certificate for him had remained in the lost file of the Presiding Bishopric's Office for many years.

On Sunday morning Elizabeth Keachie brought to our priesthood meeting Charles and William Ringwood. This was the first time they had been inside a chapel for a long while. Charles Ringwood was the oldest deacon I had ever met. His son was the oldest male member holding no priesthood I had ever met.

Brother Charles Ringwood was ordained a priest and then an elder. I shall never forget his interview with respect to seeking a temple recommend. He handed me a silver dollar, which he took from an old, worn leather coin purse, and said, "This is my fast offering."

I said, "Brother Ringwood, you owe no fast offering. You need it yourself."

"I want to receive the blessings, not retain the money," he responded.

It was my opportunity to take Charles Ringwood to the Salt Lake Temple and to attend with him the endowment session. That evening Elizabeth Keachie served as proxy for the deceased Mrs. Ringwood.

At the conclusion of the ceremony, Charles Ringwood said to me, "I told my wife just before she died sixteen years ago that I would not delay in getting this work done. I am happy this has been accomplished."

Within two months, Charles W. Ringwood passed away. At his funeral service, I noticed his family sitting on the front row of the White Chapel Mortuary in Salt Lake City, but I also noticed two sweet ladies sitting near the rear of the chapel, Elizabeth Keachie and Helen Ivory. As I gazed upon those two sweet women, I thought of the seventy-sixth section of the Doctrine and Covenants: "I, the Lord, am merciful and gracious unto those who fear me, and delight to honor those who serve me in righteousness and in truth unto the end. Great shall be their reward and eternal shall be their glory." (D&C 76:5-6.)

A Delayed Hospital Visit

One evening in 1951, when I served as bishop of the Sixth-Seventh Ward, I received a telephone call from a former schoolmate of mine at the University of Utah. He advised me that his uncle, Brother Brown, was seriously ill in the Veterans Hospital. Since Brother Brown lived in my ward, although inactive, his nephew asked if I would find time to go to the hospital and give him a blessing. This I agreed to do.

On that particular night, we had our stake priesthood meeting, followed by stake priesthood leadership meeting. My obligation was clear. I would attend my meetings and then visit the hospital.

I found it extremely difficult to sit through the first meeting, for I felt strongly that I should be at the Veterans Hospital at the side of Brother Brown. When the first meeting adjourned, I told my counselors to kindly excuse me from the second meeting—that I must go to the hospital, which I did.

When I arrived at the hospital, I rushed to the information desk and ascertained the number of Brother Brown's room. Not waiting for the elevator, I ran upstairs.

I arrived at his room just as the attending doctor pulled the sheet over his face. The nurse said, "Could you be Bishop Monson?"

"Yes, ma'am," I replied.

She said, "He was calling your name when he died."

I left the hospital with a determination in my heart that when conflicts of duty appear, an essential visit must take precedence over a scheduled meeting. I learned also this truth: *Never postpone a prompting of the Spirit.*

Blessing at a Baptism

Robert, who stuttered and stammered, void of control, was a priest in my ward when I was bishop. Self-conscious, shy, fearful of himself and all others, he had an impediment of speech that was devastating to him. Never did he fulfill an assignment; never would he look another in the eye; always would he gaze downward. Then one day, through a set of unusual circumstances, he accepted an assignment to perform the priestly responsibility to baptize another.

I sat next to him in the baptistry of the Salt Lake Tabernacle. He was dressed in immaculate white, prepared for the ordinance he was to perform. I asked Robert how he felt. He gazed at the floor and stuttered almost incoherently that he felt terrible.

We both prayed fervently that he would be made equal to his task. Then the clerk read the words: "Nancy Ann McArthur will now be baptized by Robert Williams, a priest." Robert left my side, stepped into the font, took little Nancy by the hand, and helped her into that water which cleanses human lives and provides a spiritual rebirth. He then gazed as though toward heaven and, with his right arm to the square, repeated the words, "Nancy Ann McArthur, having been commissioned of Jesus Christ, I baptize you in the name of the Father, and of the Son, and of the Holy Ghost." Not once did he stammer. Not once did he stutter. Not once did he falter. A modern miracle had been witnessed.

In the dressing room, as I congratulated Robert, I expected to hear this same uninterrupted flow of speech. I was wrong. He gazed downward and stammered his reply of gratitude. But during that moment when Robert acted in the authority of the Aaronic Priesthood, he spoke with power, with conviction, and with Heavenly help.

Christmas Gifts with Meaning

§**🙥**

At Christmastime, during my first year as a bishop, I received a telephone call from the teacher of a Mutual Improvement Association class in one of the more affluent wards on the east bench of Salt Lake City. Representing her entire MIA, she asked if there were any poor among our ward, people who needed a "Sub for Santa." I responded that there were some in our ward of scanty means and indicated I had one particular family in mind and that perhaps an experience could be planned that would benefit the young people in her ward as well as this particular family. She agreed.

Within days I provided her with the names, sizes, ages, and needs of the many children in the family, as well as the parents. I suggested that if each boy or girl could bring to the family on the appointed night a gift that meant a great deal to him or to her personally, then each would have a Christmas that would long be remembered.

The appointed evening arrived, and into the parking lot of the Sixth-Seventh Ward came one Buick, one Cadillac, and two Oldsmobiles. Such an array of wealth had never before graced that parking area. The cars were left at the chapel. We walked to the home, singing carols along the way.

We knocked at the door of the humble home. Two grateful parents welcomed us in. A little fire glowed in the fireplace, casting its light against the small Christmas tree. At this tiny home between Fourth and Fifth South on Second West Street, the Christmas spirit truly entered each heart.

One girl handed to one of the daughters a lovely doll that she had kept from her childhood. She showed the tiny girl how to caress the doll and to hold it ever so tenderly in her arms. One of the boys handed to one of the sons his baseball glove, carrying Lou Gehrig's signature. The pocket of the mitt had been well worked with oil. He then explained to the young boy how to catch a baseball. Each gift was lovingly given and gratefully received.

This choice German family, so recently come from war's deprivation, simply could not believe that all these gifts were for them. *"Danke, danke, danke,"* each of them repeated; then in English, "Thank you, thank you, thank you." Tears flowed; embraces followed.

We returned to the ward, where we had a prayer together before our guests departed. I don't recall the words of that prayer, but I will never forget the spirit of it. Nor will those young people. They thanked God for this most joyous Christmas.

An Inspired Visit

§

As a bishop, I worried about any members who were inactive, not attending, not serving. Such was my thought one day as I drove down the street where Ben and Emily lived. Aches and pains of advancing years had caused them to withdraw from activity to the shelter of their home—isolated, detached, shut out from the mainstream of daily life and association. Ben and Emily had not been in our sacrament meeting for many years. Ben, a former bishop, would sit in his front room reading the New Testament.

I was en route from my uptown sales office to our plant on Industrial Road. For some reason I had driven down First West, a street I never had traveled before to reach the destination of our plant. Then I felt the unmistakable prompting to park my car and visit Ben and Emily, even though I was on my way to a meeting. I did not heed the impression at first but drove on for two more blocks; however, when the impression came again, I returned to their home.

It was a sunny weekday afternoon. I approached the door to their home and knocked. I heard the tiny fox terrier bark at my approach. Emily welcomed me in. Upon seeing me—her bishop—she exclaimed, "All day long I have waited for my phone to ring. It has been silent. I hoped that the postman would deliver a letter. He brought only bills. Bishop, how did you know today is my birthday?"

I answered, "God knows, Emily, for He loves you."

In the quiet of their living room, I said to Ben and

Emily, "I don't know why I was directed here today, but our Heavenly Father knows. Let's kneel in prayer and ask Him why." This we did, and the answer came. As we arose from our knees, I said to Brother Fullmer, "Ben, would you come to priesthood meeting in two weeks and relate to our Aaronic Priesthood the story you once told me of how you and a group of boys were en route to the Jordan River to swim one Sunday, but you felt the Spirit direct you to attend Sunday School? One of the boys who failed to respond to that prompting drowned that Sunday. Our boys would like to hear your testimony."

"I'll do it," he responded.

I then said to Sister Fullmer, "Emily, I know you have a beautiful voice. My mother has told me so. Our ward conference is a few weeks away, and our choir will sing. Would you join the choir and attend our ward conference and perhaps sing a solo?"

"What will the number be?" she inquired.

"I don't know," I said, "but I'd like you to sing it."

She sang. He spoke. Hearts were gladdened by the return to activity of Ben and Emily. They rarely missed a sacrament meeting from that day to the time each was called home. The language of the Spirit had been spoken. It had been heard. It had been understood. Hearts were touched and souls saved.

A Visit to a Grease Pit

§

One Sunday morning during the time I served as a bishop, I noted that one of our priests, Richard, was missing from the priesthood meeting. I left the quorum in the care of the adviser and visited Richard's home. His mother said he was working at the West Temple Garage. I drove to the garage in search of Richard and looked everywhere, but could not find him. Just as I was about to leave, I had the inspiration to gaze down into the old-fashioned grease pit situated at the side of the station. From the darkness I could see two shining eyes. Then I heard Richard say, "You found me, Bishop! Come on in."

I got down into the pit and said, "Richard, we missed you at church today. We love you, and we need you there." Richard agreed to come the following Sunday, no doubt hoping that this would end our conversation.

A couple of days later, Richard was back at work when he had an accident. He slipped while emerging from the pit and cut his chin badly. He later told me that at that moment all he could think about was our conversation. He remembered the words, "We love you, and we need you there." When he recovered from his injury, he returned to church and became completely active.

The family moved to a nearby stake, and Richard moved with them. Time passed, and I received a phone call informing me that Richard was responding to a mission call to Mexico. I was invited by the family to speak at his farewell testimonial. At the meeting, when Richard responded, he mentioned that the turning point in his determination to fill a mission came from a Sunday morning visit when he gazed up from the depths of a dark grease pit and found his quorum president's outstretched hand.

Through the years I have received occasional progress reports from "the boy in the grease pit," telling of his testimony, his family, and his faithful service in the Church, including his service as a bishop himself. In January 1994 I received the following note from him:

> *Dear President Monson:*
>
> *I wanted to let you know that the boy in the grease pit is fine and still true to the faith. My testimony of the gospel grows each day more and more. My love for the Lord and Savior also grows more and more each day.*
>
> *As I ponder the events in my life, I am so grateful for a bishop who looked for me, found me and showed a great interest in me—one who was lost. I thank you from the bottom of my heart for all that you did and have done for me personally—and for your counsel, your love, and your concern.*
>
> *Richard*

Home Teaching and a German Dog

One Sunday afternoon I received a telephone call from Kaspar J. Fetzer, who served as a member of the high council of the Temple View Stake, with his specific assignment being home teaching. His voice was cheerful as he spoke with a thick German accent. He said, "Bishop Monson, I thank you for having your home teaching report in on time." Now, I knew this was simply an introduction; my report was always submitted on time. He continued, "Bishop, I don't understand the line on the report where you say you have twelve families that are inaccessible. What does that word mean?"

I explained that these were persons who rejected our home teachers, who wanted nothing to do with the Church.

"*Vat?!*" he countered. "They do not want the priesthood of God to visit them?"

"That's correct," I assured him.

Brother Fetzer then asked, "Bishop, could I please come to your home and obtain the names of these families and visit them as your helper?" I was overjoyed. I had been a bishop for five years and had met many high councilors, but this was the first time one of them had volunteered to do such personal work.

Brother Fetzer arrived within the hour, and I provided him a list of the names and addresses of those I had shown as being inaccessible. I had arranged the list with the most difficult family first, for I wanted my judgment to be vindicated.

Off he went with his special list, calling first on the

Reinhold Doelle family, a family that lived in a spacious home, perhaps the loveliest in the ward. The home had a white picket fence that enclosed the large yard of grass and flowers, a yard carefully patrolled by a German shepherd guard dog, which barked or growled at any intruder a readily recognizable message: "Stay out!" Many years earlier, Brother Doelle had had a falling out with his home teacher, who was an Englishman. They had argued over World War I, and in that particular situation, the German side had emerged victorious. Home teachers had not been allowed in the home since that time.

Brother Fetzer checked his listing against the address that appeared on the house, left his car, and walked toward the gate. As he reached over the top of the gate to release the catch, he saw the big German shepherd dog charging at him. And the dog meant business! Instantly, Brother Fetzer exclaimed in his native German some message to the dog that caused it to come to a halt. He stroked the back of the dog and spoke softly in German, a language the dog's master used when speaking to it. The dog's tail began to wag, the gate was unlocked, and that home had a visit from a home teacher—the first such visit in many years.

Later that Sunday afternoon, Brother Fetzer returned to my home and, with a smile, reported, "Bishop, you can cross from your inaccessible list seven of these families, who will now welcome the home teachers."

A lesson had been taught. A lesson had been learned. A truth had been verified: *Where there is a will, there is a way.*

Long years after this incident, I was waiting in a wedding reception line to enter the home of a prominent family in Salt Lake City. A woman standing in line before me turned and greeted me. I recognized her as Sister Doelle from my old ward. She said the family lived now in

California and that Brother Doelle had passed away. Then she said, "I wonder what ever became of that wonderful home teacher, Brother Fetzer, who called at our home when we lived in your ward. His visit changed our lives. We determined then and there to mend our ways and become active in the Church. Why, today I am in the presidency of our Relief Society in Palm Springs. We shall always be grateful for that special visit from a very special home teacher."

While Kaspar Fetzer had gone to his eternal reward, I am certain he would have been pleased with the result of that visit.

Above the Hinges

When Kaspar J. Fetzer was appointed chairman of the
stake home teaching committee of Temple View Stake,
home teaching was at a low ebb. Our stake average was
approximately 64 percent. I was bishop of the Sixth-
Seventh Ward at the time.

Brother Fetzer, in his own ingenious way, devised a
large board upon which he would show a listing of each
ward and the home teaching percentage achieved that particular month. The size of the board required that it be
hinged along the center.

Under the direction of President Adiel F. Stewart,
Brother Fetzer was given a brief period of time at every
stake priesthood or stake priesthood leadership meeting to
comment relative to home teaching.

When Brother Fetzer first unveiled the board, Glen
Rudd, who was bishop of the Fourth Ward, leaned over to
me, as he noted that our ward was listed on the bottom
half, and said, "Tom, are you below the hinges?"

The comment caught on, and no bishop wanted to be
"below the hinges." At first, to be above the hinges, one
needed to have only 65 percent home teaching, but then it
rose to 70 and then 75 and then 80; finally our stake
achieved 90 percent home teaching. On this night, Kaspar
Fetzer took masking tape and covered the hinges and said
to the priesthood, "Tonight no ward in the Temple View
Stake is below the hinges."

Collecting Fast Offerings

In many areas, fast offerings are collected each month by the boys who are deacons, as they visit each member's home, generally quite early on the Sabbath day. I recall that the boys in the congregation over which I presided as bishop had assembled one morning sleepy-eyed, a bit disheveled, and mildly complaining about arising so early to fulfill their assignment.

Not a word of reproof was spoken, but during the following week, we escorted the boys to Welfare Square for a guided tour. They saw firsthand a disabled person operating the telephone switchboard, an older man stocking shelves, women arranging clothing to be distributed—even a blind person placing labels on cans. Here were individuals earning their sustenance through their contributed labors.

A penetrating silence came over the boys as they were taught how their efforts each month helped to collect the sacred fast offering funds, which aided the needy and provided employment for those who otherwise would be idle.

From that hallowed day forward, there was no urging required with our deacons. On fast Sunday mornings they were present, dressed in their Sunday best, anxious to do their duty as holders of the Aaronic Priesthood. No longer were they simply distributing and collecting envelopes. They were helping to provide food for the hungry and shelter for the homeless—all after the way of the Lord. Their smiles were more frequent, their pace more eager, their very souls more subdued.

Leaving the Ninety and Nine

When I was a bishop, I received a telephone call from Elder Spencer W. Kimball. He said, "Brother Monson, in your ward is a trailer court, and in a little trailer in that court—the smallest trailer of all—is a sweet Navajo widow, Margaret Bird. She feels unwanted, unneeded, and lost. Could you and the Relief Society presidency seek her out, extend to her the hand of fellowship, and provide for her a special welcome?" This we did.

A miracle resulted. Margaret Bird blossomed in her newly found environment. Despair disappeared. The widow in her affliction had been visited. The lost sheep had been found. Each who participated in the simple human drama emerged a better person.

In reality, the true shepherd was the concerned apostle, Spencer W. Kimball, who, leaving the ninety and nine of his ministry, went in search of the precious soul who was lost.

The Finest Coal Shed

❧

One cold winter day I visited an elderly couple who lived in a two-room duplex in my ward. The modest home was heated by a small coal-burning Heatrola. As I approached the home, I met the husband, his aged body bent in the driving snow as he gathered a few pieces of wet coal from his exposed supply of fuel. I helped him fill the bucket, and then we took it inside and attempted to start a fire in the stove of that cold house. I said to him, "How long have you had wet coal?" He replied, "Bishop, I've never had dry coal in the winter."

Later in the evening, as I pondered and prayed and sought for a way to help this fine couple, the inspiration came. In our ward was a carpenter who was temporarily out of work. He had no fuel for his furnace but was too proud to receive the coal slack he needed to keep his house warm. I telephoned him and said, "We need you to build a coal shed, but I won't let you do it unless you permit me to arrange for four tons of slack to be delivered to your house from Deseret Coal."

He said, "Well, when you put it that way, I suppose I can't refuse."

Now where were we to obtain the materials for the shed? I approached the proprietors of a local lumberyard from whom we frequently purchased products. I remember saying to the men, "How would the two of you like to paint a bright spot on your souls this winter day?" Not knowing exactly what I meant, they agreed readily. They were invited to donate the lumber and hardware for the coal shed.

Within days the project was completed. I was invited to inspect the outcome. The coal shed was simply beautiful in its sleek covering of battleship-gray paint. The carpenter, who was a high priest, testified that he had actually felt inspired as he labored on this modest shed.

My older friend, the recipient of the carpenter's labors, stroked the wall of the sturdy structure with obvious appreciation. He pointed out to me the wide door, the shiny hinges, and then opened to my view the supply of dry coal that filled the shed. In a voice filled with emotion, he said, in words I shall ever treasure, "Bishop, take a look at the finest coal shed a man ever had." Its beauty was only surpassed by the pride in the builder's heart. And the elderly recipient labored each day at the ward chapel, dusting the benches, vacuuming the carpet runners, arranging the hymnbooks. He too worked for that which he had received.

Once again, the welfare plan of the Lord had blessed the lives of His children.

A Family Project

I recall an elderly couple whose frame home, situated at the end of a dirt lane, had not seen a coat of paint for too many years. These were neat and tidy people; they were concerned about the appearance of their small house but were unable to pay to have the house painted and were not able to do it themselves. In a moment of inspiration, as their bishop, I called not upon the elders quorum or upon volunteers to wield paint brushes, but rather, following the welfare handbook, upon the family members who lived in other areas.

Four sons-in-law and four daughters took brushes in hand and participated in the project. The paint had been provided by a dealer located in our area. The result was a transformation not only of the house but also of the family. The children determined how they might best help their parents in their old age. They did so voluntarily and with gladness of heart. A house was painted, a family united, and respect preserved.

A Better Christmas Party

In New York City at one time, there presided over one of the stakes of the Church a young man who, as a boy of thirteen, had led his quorum of deacons in a successful search for the Christmas spirit. Frank and his companions lived in a neighborhood in which resided many elderly widows of limited means. All year long, the boys had saved and planned for a glorious Christmas party. They were thinking of themselves until the Christmas spirit prompted them to think of others. Frank suggested to his companions that the funds they had accumulated so carefully be used not for the planned party, but for the benefit of three elderly widows who resided together. The boys made their plans. As their bishop, I needed but to follow.

With the enthusiasm of a new adventure, the boys purchased a giant roasting chicken, the potatoes, the vegetables, the cranberries, and all that comprises the traditional Christmas feast. To the widows' home they went, carrying their gifts of treasure. Through the snow and up the path to the tumbledown porch they came. A knock at the door, the sound of slow footsteps, and then they met.

In the unmelodic voices characteristic of thirteen-year-olds, the boys sang "Silent night, holy night; all is calm, all is bright." They then presented their gifts. Angels on that glorious night of long ago sang no more beautifully, nor did wise men present gifts of greater meaning.

As a silent observer, I gazed at the faces of those wonderful women, and I then looked on the countenances of those noble boys. What was the message of the Master? "Inasmuch as ye have done it unto one of the least of these, . . . ye have done it unto me." (Matthew 25:40.)

The Other Hospital Bed

Many years ago when I was a bishop, I went to the old county hospital in Salt Lake City to visit a member of our ward, Mary Watson, who had just entered the hospital. As I entered that large hospital ward, I headed toward the bed where I had been told she would be. As I approached her, I noted that the person in the bed next to her pulled the sheet up over her face. I assumed that she wanted privacy. So I visited with Mary Watson for a while and then gave her a priesthood blessing.

After bestowing that blessing, I said good-bye to her and had taken just about two steps when I felt compelled by the Holy Spirit to turn around and walk over to that bed where the woman had pulled the sheet over her face. I tapped her on the arm and pulled the sheet back just a little bit. How surprised I was to find that here was another member of my ward who I had not known was even in the hospital. I said to her, "Sister McKee, I didn't know you were here."

Then she cried and said, "When I saw you coming through that door, Bishop, I said, 'My goodness, my bishop has come to give me a blessing.' And then when I saw you stop at the bedside of Mary Watson, I was so embarrassed about thinking you had come to see me, when in reality you had not, that I pulled the sheet over my face so that I would not intrude on your time."

I said to her, "Sister McKee, I may not have known that you were here, but the Lord knew you were here." Another blessing was provided.

That night I expressed in my personal prayer my

gratitude to our Heavenly Father, who had not failed to remember the needy in their affliction. But then, doesn't He always remember them? He may do so in ways that we do not at times fully understand, but He does remember.

A Paper Boat and Guidance

§▲

When I think of the influence of a single good man upon a boy, I think of an experience of Louis C. Jacobsen. He served the Church as a bishop and a high councilor. He served his community as a Scouter, a member of service clubs for boys. He was a successful industrialist, a master in the art of working with others, a father of boys. He ministered to those in need, he assisted the immigrant to find employment, and he delivered more sermons at more funeral services than any other person I have known.

One day while in a reflective mood, Louis Jacobsen told me of his boyhood. He was the son of a poor Danish widow. He was small in stature, not comely in appearance—easily the object of his classmates' thoughtless jokes. In Sunday School one Sabbath morning, the children made light of his patched trousers and his worn shirt. Too proud to cry, tiny Louis fled from the chapel, stopping at last, out of breath, to sit and rest on the curb that ran along Second West Street in Salt Lake City. Clear water flowed along the gutter next to the curb where Louis sat. From his pocket he took a piece of paper that contained the outlined Sunday School lesson and skillfully shaped a paper boat, which he launched on the flowing water. From his hurt boyish heart came the determined words, "I'll never go back."

Suddenly, through his tears, Louis saw reflected in the water the image of a large and well-dressed man. Louis turned his face upward and recognized George Burbidge, the Sunday School superintendent.

"May I sit down with you?" asked the kind leader.

Louis nodded affirmatively. There on the gutter's curb

sat a good Samaritan ministering to one who surely was in need. Several boats were formed and launched while the conversation continued. At last the leader stood, and, with a boy's hand tightly clutching his, they returned to Sunday School.

Later Louis himself presided over that same Sunday School. Throughout his long life of service, he never failed to acknowledge the friend who rescued him. A boy had come to the crossroads of decision; a leader was there to guide him.

A Surprised Member

꙳

Some years ago, I served as president of the Canadian Mission. At that time the North Bay Branch, which was located some 250 miles north of our headquarters in Toronto, was a struggling unit desperately in need of priesthood leadership. When I attended that branch and recognized this fact, I held an interview with Brother Mabey. He had moved his family from Salt Lake City to North Bay, Ontario, because of a business transfer by his company. He was an elder in the Church but had been less than fully active in priesthood callings. He was about thirty-five years of age at the time.

I said to him, "I am calling you to serve as the president of the North Bay Branch."

He replied, "I can't do it."

I asked, "Why?"

He answered, "I have never done it before."

"That's no hindrance," I responded. I took fresh hope from his name, Mabey, and the words of a once-popular ballad, "Please don't say no—say maybe."

Brother Mabey said yes. He presided in dignity over the North Bay Branch. He later became a high priest, and all of his family members entered temple doors and received temple blessings.

A Response to the Spirit

Once at Christmas time, I was returning home from an activity on a street that I very seldom traveled. As I proceeded eastward on California Avenue, I happened to think, "In one of these houses there resides a family that lived in our ward when I was bishop long years ago. I wonder how Sister Thomas is getting along." I drove right on by, hurriedly anticipating my next appointment. But then the Spirit seemed to indicate to me, "Why don't you go back, Brother Monson, and find out how Sister Thomas is getting along?"

I turned the car around, found the house, pulled into the driveway, and knocked at the door. No one answered. I knocked again. Still no answer. I returned to the automobile and was ready to back out onto the street when someone appeared at the doorway. As I again walked to the door, I beheld a lovely, silver-haired woman with whom I had served in the Mutual Improvement Association years before, Sister Zella Thomas. I extended my hand and said, "Sister Thomas, it is good to see you. How are you?" Her hand seemed to grope for mine.

She said, "I know the voice, but I can't see you. I'm blind." Only then did I appreciate why the Lord had directed me to bring a Christmas greeting to this sweet friend of years ago and to her family. As I talked to her and to her family members, I found that on that particular day she happened to be remembering the anniversary of the death of her eldest daughter. She particularly needed comfort from one holding the priesthood of God. How grateful I was for the opportunity to respond to the directional influence of our Heavenly Father.

Help for a Humble Home

❧

Situated beneath the heavily traveled freeway that girds Salt Lake City was the home of a sixty-year-old single man who, due to a crippling disease, had never known a day without pain nor many days without loneliness. One winter's day as I visited him, he was slow in answering the doorbell's ring. I entered his well-kept home; the temperature in save but one room—the kitchen—was a chilly 40 degrees. The reason: not sufficient money to heat any other room. The walls needed papering, the ceilings needed to be lowered, the cupboards needed to be filled.

I was troubled by the experience of visiting my friend. A bishop was consulted, and a miracle of love, prompted by testimony, took place. The ward members were organized and the labor of love begun.

A month later, my friend, whose name was Louis, called and asked if I would come and see what had happened to him. I did and indeed beheld a miracle. The sidewalks that had been uprooted by large poplar trees had been replaced, the porch of the home rebuilt, a new door with glistening hardware installed, the ceilings lowered, the walls papered, the woodwork painted, the roof replaced, and the cupboards filled. No longer was the home chilly and uninviting. It now seemed to whisper a warm welcome.

Louis saved until last showing me his pride and joy: there on his bed was a beautiful plaid quilt bearing the crest of his McDonald family clan. It had been made with loving care by the women of the Relief Society. Before leaving, I discovered that each week the Young Adults would bring in a hot dinner and share a home evening. Warmth had replaced the cold; repairs had transformed the wear of years; but more significantly, hope had dispelled despair and now love reigned triumphant.

All who participated in this moving drama of real life had discovered a new and personal appreciation of the Master's teaching, "It is more blessed to give than to receive." (Acts 20:35.)

Twenty-three Years of Service

Some years ago I was in Star Valley, Wyoming, to effect a reorganization of the stake presidency there. The stake president at the time was the late E. Francis Winters. He had served faithfully for the lengthy term of twenty-three years. Though modest by nature and circumstance, he had been a perpetual pillar of strength to everyone in the valley. On the day of the stake conference, the building was filled to overflowing. Each heart seemed to be saying a silent thank-you to this noble leader who had given so unselfishly of his life for the benefit of others.

As I stood to speak following the reorganization of the stake presidency, I was prompted to do something I had not done before. I stated how long Francis Winters had presided in the stake; then I asked all whom he had blessed or confirmed as children to stand and remain standing. Then I asked all those persons whom President Winters had ordained, set apart, personally counseled, or blessed to please stand. The outcome was electrifying. Every person in the audience rose to his feet. Tears flowed freely—tears that communicated better than could words the gratitude of tender hearts. I turned to President and Sister Winters and said, "We are witnesses today of the prompting of the Spirit. This vast throng reflects not only individual feelings but also the gratitude of God for a life well-lived."

A Loaned Jacket

On one occasion I attended the sacrament meeting of a small branch that consisted of patients in a nursing home. Most of the members were elderly and somewhat incapacitated. During the service, a sister called out aloud, "I'm cold! I'm cold!" Without so much as a glance, one of the priests at the sacrament table arose and walked over to this sister, removed his suit coat, placed it around her shoulders, and then returned to his duties at the sacrament table.

After the meeting, he came to me and apologized for blessing the sacrament without his suit coat. Quietly, I said to him that he was never more appropriately dressed than he was that day when a dear widow was uncomfortably cold and he provided the warmth she needed by placing his jacket around her shoulders. A simple act of kindness? Yes, but much more—evidence of a genuine love and concern for others.

A Swimming Pool and a Wheelchair

Stan, a dear friend of mine, was taken seriously ill and rendered partially paralyzed. He had been robust in health, athletic in build, and active in many pursuits. Now he was unable to walk or to stand. His wheelchair was his home. The finest of physicians had cared for him, and the prayers of family and friends had been offered in a spirit of hope and trust. Yet Stan continued to lie in the confinement of his bed at the university hospital. He despaired.

Late one afternoon I was swimming at the Deseret Gym, gazing at the ceiling while backstroking width after width. Silently, but ever so clearly, there came to my mind the thought: "Here you swim almost effortlessly, while your friend Stan languishes in his hospital bed, unable to move." I felt the prompting: "Get to the hospital and give him a blessing."

I ceased my swimming, dressed, and hurried to Stan's room at the hospital. His bed was empty. A nurse said he was in his wheelchair at the swimming pool, preparing for therapy. I hurried to the area, and there was Stan, all alone, at the edge of the deeper portion of the pool. We greeted one another and returned to his room, where a priesthood blessing was provided.

Slowly but surely, strength and movement returned to Stan's legs. First he could stand on faltering feet. Then he learned once again to walk—step by step.

Following his recovery, Stan frequently spoke in church meetings and told of the goodness of the Lord to him. Sometimes he revealed the dark thoughts of depression that engulfed him that afternoon as he sat in his wheelchair at the edge of the pool, sentenced, it seemed, to a life of despair—and how he pondered the alternative. It would be so easy to propel the hated wheelchair into the silent water of the deep pool. Life would then be over. But at that precise moment he saw me, his friend. That day Stan learned literally that we do not walk alone. I too learned a lesson that day: Never postpone heeding a prompting.

A Long-Awaited Son

Each time I would visit Mattie, a dear friend and an older widow whom I had known for many years and whose bishop I had been, my heart grieved at her utter loneliness. One of her sons lived many miles away, halfway across the country, but he never visited her. He would come to Salt Lake City, take care of business matters, see his brothers and sisters, and leave for his home without visiting his mother. When I would call to see this mother, who was a widow, she would make an excuse for her boy and tell me just how busy he was. Her words did not carry power or conviction. They simply masked her disappointment and grief.

The years passed. The loneliness deepened. Then one afternoon I received a telephone call. That special son was in Salt Lake City. A change had occurred in his life. He had become imbued with a desire to help others, to adhere more faithfully to God's commandments. He was proud of his newfound ability to cast off the old man and become new and useful. He wanted to come immediately to my office so that he might share with me the joy in service that he now felt. With all my heart I wanted to welcome him and to extend my personal congratulations. Then I thought of his grieving mother, that lonely widow, and suggested, "Dick, I can see you at four o'clock this afternoon, provided you visit your dear mother before coming here." He agreed.

Just before our appointment, a call came to me. It was that same mother. There was an excitement in her voice that words cannot adequately describe. She exuded enthusiasm even over the phone, and declared proudly, "Bishop, you'll never guess who has just visited me." Before I could answer, she exclaimed, "Dick was here! My son Dick has spent the past hour with me. He is a new man. He has found himself. I'm the happiest mother in the world!" Then she paused and quietly said, "I just knew he would not really forget me."

Years later at Mattie's funeral, Dick and I spoke tenderly of that experience. We had witnessed a glimpse of God's healing power through the window of a mother's faith in her son.

An Evening with Jane

As the Christmas season approached one year, a teacher of sixteen-year-old Laurel girls arranged a visit to bring joy to the heart of a lonely widow, Jane. I had served as Jane's bishop many years before. The girls busied themselves preparing delicious cookies, special refreshments, even a Christmas tree with ornaments to be placed thereon. They did not forget a beautiful corsage, which they knew would brighten the spirit of the special widow they planned to visit.

With their parcels tucked tightly under each arm, the girls and their teacher made their way up the never-ending flights of stairs that led to Jane's apartment. I was privileged to accompany them. There was an interminable delay as aged feet made their way to the door. Then came the tedious task of unbolting the door. Lonely people fear the dark, the unknown, and lock and counterlock the door to home. Some similarly lock and counterlock the door to the soul, fearful of being disappointed or deeply hurt.

The door opened, and beautiful young women were made welcome in the humble apartment. Their smiles reflected the goodness of their hearts as they erected the Christmas tree and placed upon it the decorations they had so carefully carried. Then the packaged gifts were placed beneath its outstretched branches. I had never seen a more beautiful tree, for no tree had ever before been decorated with such love, such Christlike care and concern. The teacher slipped into the kitchen, and with the aid of three of the girls, the refreshments were prepared and a feast enjoyed.

Then this dear widow gathered the girls around her to share with them her life's memories. She told how, as a young girl in far-off Scotland, she had heard the missionaries, embraced the truth that they taught—even suffered the jibes and comments that adherence to a then unpopular faith inevitably provoked. She told them how the entire Sabbath day was taken just to travel and to attend the meetings of her newfound faith. Instinctively the girls compared her account with the ease with which they made their way each Sunday to their chapel.

When Jane told them of the voyage to America, described the storm-tossed Atlantic and the warm feeling that came to her heart when the Statue of Liberty was first glimpsed, I noted that the girls were visibly touched. Tears brimmed in their eyes, and pledges were made within their hearts, pledges to do that which is correct, to be honorable, to live true to the faith.

As the evening came to an end, there were kisses and embraces, and then each girl filed silently from the doorway and made her way down the stairs to the street outside. They left behind a mother filled with the goodness of the world, with love rekindled, with faith again inspired. I'm certain this was one of the happiest days of her life. That night the corsage was carefully and tenderly placed in safekeeping. It had become a symbol of all that is good and clean and wholesome.

Honoring a Former Leader

Many years ago I was assigned to divide the Modesto California Stake. The Saturday meetings had been held, the new stake presidencies selected, and preparations concluded for the announcements to be made the following morning in the Sunday session of conference.

That Sunday morning, as the session was about to begin, there went through my mind the thought that I had been in Modesto before. But when? As I searched my memory, the thought came to me that Modesto, years before, had been a part of the San Joaquin Stake. The stake president was Clifton Rooker, and I had stayed in his home during that conference. But that was many years earlier, and I wasn't certain I was remembering correctly. I said to members of the stake presidency as they sat on the stand, "Was this stake formerly the San Joaquin Stake, where Clifton Rooker once presided?"

The brethren answered, "Yes, it is. He was stake president some years ago."

"It's been many years since I was last here," I said. "Is Brother Rooker with us today?"

They responded, "Oh, yes. We saw him early this morning as he came to conference."

I asked where he was seated. "We don't know exactly," they replied. The building was filled to capacity.

I stepped to the pulpit and asked, "Is Clifton Rooker in the audience?" There he was—way back in the cultural hall, hardly in view of the pulpit. I felt the inspiration to say to him publicly, "Brother Rooker, we have a place for you on the stand. Would you please come forward?"

With every eye watching him, Clifton Rooker made that long walk from the rear of the building right up to the front and sat by my side. It became my opportunity to call upon him, one of the pioneers of that stake, to bear his testimony and to tell the people whom he loved that he was the actual beneficiary of the service he had rendered his Heavenly Father and that he had provided the stake members.

After the session was concluded, I said, "Brother Rooker, how would you like to step with me into the high council room and help me set apart the two new presidencies of these stakes?"

He replied, "That would be a highlight for me."

We proceeded to the high council room. There, with his hands joining my hands and the hands of the outgoing stake presidency, we set apart to their callings the two new stake presidencies. Brother Rooker and I embraced as he said good-bye and went to his home.

Just a few days later, after I had returned to Salt Lake City, I had a telephone call from the son of Clifton Rooker. "Brother Monson," he said, "I'd like to tell you about my dad. He passed away this morning, but before he did so, he said that conference last Sunday was one of the happiest days of his entire life."

As I heard that message from Brother Rooker's son, I paused to thank God for the inspiration that came to me to invite this good man, while he was yet alive and able to enjoy them, to come forward and receive the plaudits of the stake members whom he had served.

Missionary Joseph A. Ott Remembered

&

In distant Dresden, Germany, a city then situated behind an iron curtain and far from freedom's friendly face, I visited a small cemetery on October 22, 1978, with a handful of Church members. The night was dark, and a cold rain had been falling throughout the day.

We had come to visit the grave of a missionary who many years before had died while in the service of the Lord. A hushed silence shrouded the scene as we gathered about the grave. With a flashlight illuminating the headstone, I read the inscription:

Joseph A. Ott
Born: 12 December 1870–Virgin, Utah
Died: 10 January 1896–Dresden, Germany

Then the light revealed that this grave was unlike any other in the cemetery. The headstone had been polished, weeds such as those that covered other graves had been carefully removed, and in their place was an immaculately edged bit of lawn and some beautiful flowers that told of tender and loving care. I asked, "Who has made this grave so attractive?" My query was met by silence.

At length an eleven-year-old boy, Tobias Burkhardt, acknowledged that he had wanted to render this unheralded kindness and, without prompting from parents or leaders, had done so. He said that he just wanted to do something for a missionary who gave his life while in the service of the Lord. He said, "I'll never be able to serve a mission as did my father. I feel close to missionary work when I tend this grave where the body of a missionary

rests." I wept out of respect for his faith. I sorrowed at his inability to fulfill his greatest desire—to serve as a missionary. But God did hear his prayer. He noted his faith.

Nearly eleven years after that special night in Dresden, many significant changes had taken place in that part of Germany. A temple of God graced the land. Chapels accommodated wards and stakes, and the full program of the Church blessed the lives of our members. On Thursday, March 30, 1989, the first missionaries in fifty years crossed the border into what was then the German Democratic Republic. Their message was proclaimed and was received by a prepared people. Membership in the Church began to grow.

But what of Tobias Burkhardt, who had so tenderly tended the grave of Joseph Ott? He became an elder. On May 28, 1989, he and nine other companions traveled to the Missionary Training Center in Provo, Utah—the first from their country to serve abroad as missionaries. Asked concerning his feelings at that time, he responded, "I'm anxious to serve my mission. I'll strive to work ever so diligently so that Joseph Ott can, through me, yet perform an earthly mission."

The spirit of Joseph Ott had long since gone home to that God who gave him life. His body rested in the peaceful, well-kept grave in faraway Dresden. But his missionary spirit lived on in the service rendered by a faithful elder—even a boy who so long ago had trimmed the lawn, tidied the flowers, and polished the headstone of Joseph Ott, and dreamed of missionary service once denied but now bestowed.

A Memorable Dinner

&

An example of true love and inspired teaching was found in James Collier, who had, through his personal efforts, reactivated a large number of brethren in the Bountiful area. I was invited by Brother Collier to address those who had now been ordained elders and who had just been with their wives and families to the Salt Lake Temple. Although I had planned to leave for an assignment in Germany that very day, I knew that Jim was dying of leukemia, and I couldn't turn my back on his petition. I accepted and changed my flight to the following day.

I went to Bountiful and saw Jim walking among the banquet tables and shaking hands with each brother, telling him, "I love you! I'm glad you made it! Keep up the good work!" And then he stepped to the pulpit, and silence engulfed that room. He said, "All of you here know that I'm dying. You know that I got up out of my hospital bed with the doctor's permission to come here, and after this meeting tonight I'll go back to the hospital." Tears were streaming from the eyes of those brethren and their wives. Jim continued, "You know, it's interesting about Latter-day Saints. We all want to go to the celestial kingdom, but nobody wants to die to get there." Then, in a voice filled with emotion, he said, "I'm prepared to go, and I will be there waiting on the other side to greet each of you, my beloved friends."

When the meeting was over, Jim waved good-bye and left for the hospital, where he died two days later. Those men and women will never forget that man who loved his assignment and loved the men with whom he was working, and who had the capacity to say, "I love you!"

A Priceless Scouting Skill

In 1984 a Scouting skill saved a life—in my own family. My nephew's son, eleven-year-old Craig Dearden, successfully completed his requirements for Scouting's swimming award. On the day the awards were presented, his father beamed his approval while his mother tenderly placed an affectionate kiss on his cheek. Little did those attending the Court of Honor realize the life-or-death impact of that award.

Later that very afternoon, it was Craig who spotted a dark object at the deep end of the swimming pool. It was Craig who, without fear, plunged into the pool to investigate and brought to the surface his own little brother. Tiny Scott was so still, so blue, so lifeless. Recalling the life-saving procedures he had learned and practiced, Craig, with others, responded in the true tradition of Scouting. Suddenly there was a cry, breathing, movement—life.

Is Scouting relevant? Ask a mother, a father, a family who know that a Scouting skill saved a son and brother.

An Odyssey of Redemption

The desire to help another, the quest for the lost sheep, may not always yield success at once. On occasion progress is slow, even indiscernible. Such was the experience of my longtime friend Gil Warner. He was serving as a newly called bishop when Douglas (not his name), a member of his ward, transgressed and was deprived of his Church membership. His father was saddened; his mother was totally devastated. Douglas soon thereafter moved from the state. The years hurried by, but Bishop Warner, now a member of a high council, never ceased to wonder what had become of him.

In 1975 I attended the stake conference of Brother Warner's stake and held a priesthood leadership meeting early on Sunday morning. I spoke of the Church discipline system and the need to labor earnestly and lovingly to rescue any who had strayed. Gil Warner raised his hand and outlined the story of Douglas. He concluded by posing a question to me: "Who has the responsibility to work with Douglas and bring him back to Church membership?"

Gil reminded me later that my response to his question was direct and given without hesitation: "It is your responsibility, Gil, for you were his bishop, and he knew you cared."

Unbeknownst to Gil Warner, Douglas's mother had, the previous week, fasted and prayed that a man would be raised up to help save her son. Gil discovered this when, following that meeting, he felt prompted to call her to report his determination to be of help.

Gil began his odyssey of redemption. Douglas was

contacted by him. Old times, happy times, were remembered. Testimony was expressed, love was conveyed, and confidence was instilled. The pace was excruciatingly slow. Discouragement frequently entered the scene, but step by step, Douglas made headway. At long last prayers were answered, efforts rewarded, and victory attained. Douglas was approved for baptism.

The baptismal date was set, family members gathered, and former bishop Gil Warner flew to the city where Douglas lived for the occasion. Can we appreciate the supreme joy felt by Bishop Warner as he, dressed in white, stood with Douglas in water waist-deep and, raising his right arm to the square, repeated those sacred words, "Having been commissioned of Jesus Christ, I baptize you in the name of the Father, and of the Son, and of the Holy Ghost"? (D&C 20:73.)

He that was lost was found. A twenty-six-year mission, marked by love and pursued with determination, had been successfully completed. Gil Warner said to me, "This was one of the greatest days of my life. I know the joy promised by the Lord when He declared, 'And if it so be that you should labor all your days . . . and bring, save it be one soul unto me, how great shall be your joy with him in the kingdom of my Father!'" (D&C 18:15.)

Invited by Inspiration

&.

In October of 1984, I returned from an assignment out of the state, arriving home at perhaps eight P.M. I discovered that an urgent telephone call had come from the mother and father of a young woman whose husband had been diagnosed as having a tumor on his brain. At the time he was a patient in the University Hospital. A blessing had been requested at my convenience.

My first inclination was to visit the hospital the next day, but then a prompting came ever so subtly that I should go to the hospital that very evening. Frances and I then drove through the winter snow to the University Hospital, where I was welcomed warmly by the young couple, and a blessing was provided.

As we left the hospital at about nine P.M., I paused at the exit when the thought entered my mind, "I wonder if my friend Hyrum Adams is still a patient here? It has been some months since I was here at the hospital giving him a blessing. Surely he would be discharged by now." The thought persisted, however, and after some difficulty, a custodian showed me to the switchboard area, where I inquired if Hyrum were still a patient. I was advised that indeed he was. After a difficult period of searching, I located the wing in which his room was situated.

As we approached the door to his room, and knowing that Hyrum was terminally ill with cancer, I felt that perhaps I would enter into a room of pain and quiet. Upon opening the door, however, I found just the opposite. Assembled around Hyrum's bedside were three of his sons and a son-in-law. Hyrum was in his bed in a half-lying, half-sitting position. A string extended from one corner of the room to another, from which were suspended perhaps a dozen birthday cards. On a table was a lovely birthday cake with the inscription "Happy Birthday, Dad."

Hyrum recognized me, and a great smile came over his face as he exclaimed, "Brother Monson, my friend! How in the world did you know it was my birthday?" Of course I did not know prior to entering the room that it was his birthday. I mentioned to him that the Spirit of the Lord had directed me to his bedside, and surely we should acknowledge the kindness of our Heavenly Father and provide a blessing. Hyrum's fine sons and son-in-law joined me as we surrounded Hyrum Adams and gave him a priesthood blessing.

Before leaving the room, I sang in quiet tones the traditional "Happy birthday to you," embraced Hyrum warmly, and waved good-bye. This was the last time in mortality I was to see my longtime friend. He died a month later.

At his funeral service, I recounted this special experience and mentioned to the family that surely He who notes the fall of the sparrow had noted, with great impact, that twilight of Hyrum Adams' mortal life and had provided a moment of true inspiration for all of us who were in his room that special birthday evening.

A Medal for a Brave Boy

A few years ago I was privileged to meet Evgeny Christov from Sofia, Bulgaria. His father serves in the government there. The little lad was born with a malformed urinary tract. The doctors in Romania had performed surgery on him, as had doctors in Italy, but nothing had been successful. Although the Christovs were not members of the Church, arrangements were made for Evgeny to come to Salt Lake City, where the surgeons of the Salt Lake City area would perform their skills upon him. I understand that they operated on him for the better part of a day and reconstructed his urinary tract. The doctors were able to accomplish the objective of the surgery, and they were overjoyed. They generously contributed their skills, not charging any fee—nor did the hospital.

Evgeny was later brought to my office. He couldn't say much in English. A relative was with him, as well as someone who could translate. I visited with him for a while as he sat in my office with large, sad brown eyes; he'd had so many health problems. As I looked at him, I had a ray of inspiration. I opened my desk drawer, where I had in a little blue velvet box a silver medallion I had received at the inauguration of President Rex Lee as the tenth president of Brigham Young University. I handed the box to the little boy and said, "Here is your silver medal for courage." Evgeny opened the box and looked at that silver medal in honor of Rex Lee, who also is a man of great courage. Little Evgeny broke into a beautiful smile, walked over to me, and quietly said, in his broken English, "Thank you."

Evgeny's family became one of the first families baptized and confirmed members of the Church in Bulgaria.

FAITH PRECEDES BLESSINGS

They which be of faith are blessed.

GALATIANS 3:9

Blessing in a Barracks

֎

Near the close of World War II, I joined the U.S. Navy. I turned eighteen and was ordained an elder a few weeks before I departed for active duty. A member of my ward bishopric, John R. Burt, was at the train station to bid me farewell. Just before train time, he placed in my hand two books. One was a popular satire in which I took interest. The other was the *Missionary Handbook.* I laughed and commented, "I'm not going on a mission." He answered, "Take it anyway. It may come in handy."

It did. During basic training our company commander instructed us concerning how we might best pack our clothing in a large sea bag. He advised, "If you have a hard, rectangular object you can place in the bottom of the bag, your clothes will stay more firm." I suddenly remembered just the right rectangular object: the *Missionary Handbook.* Thus it served for twelve weeks.

The night preceding our Christmas leave, our thoughts were, as always, on home. The barracks were quiet. Suddenly I became aware that my buddy in the adjoining bunk—an LDS boy, Leland Merrill—was moaning with pain. I asked, "What's the matter, Merrill?"

He replied, "I'm sick. I'm really sick."

I advised him to go to the base dispensary, but he answered knowingly that such a course would prevent him from being home for Christmas.

The hours lengthened; his groans grew louder. Then, in desperation, he whispered, "Monson, Monson, aren't you an elder?" I acknowledged this to be so, whereupon he pleaded, "Give me a blessing."

I became very much aware that I had never given a blessing. I had never received such a blessing; I had never witnessed a blessing being given. My prayer to God was a plea for help. The answer came: "Look in the bottom of the sea bag." Thus, at two A.M. I emptied on the deck the contents of the bag. I then took to the night-light that hard, rectangular object, the *Missionary Handbook,* and read how one blesses the sick. With many curious sailors looking on, I proceeded with the blessing. Before I could stow my gear, Leland Merrill was sleeping like a child.

The next morning Merrill smilingly turned to me and said, "Monson, I'm glad you hold the priesthood." His gladness was only surpassed by my gratitude.

Faith and an Old Car

&

As president of the Canadian Mission, I always enjoyed attending the North Bay District quarterly conferences, particularly when such were held at Sudbury, Ontario. The people were of rather modest means and yet were filled with faith.

Whenever the conference would convene in Sudbury, there would appear on the front row the Royden T. Fraser family. The family was composed of mother and father and three or four beautiful, blond-haired children, one of whom was lame. The children always appeared in their Sunday best and looked rubbed and scrubbed for the occasion.

Sister Fraser was quite an ardent genealogist and frequently would say, "One day, Brother Monson, we will go to the temple in Salt Lake City, so that our family may be united for all eternity." The hope seemed only a hope, or at best a dream, because the Fraser family had no car and no means to make the trip westward.

One bright spring morning in 1960, in the city of Toronto, there came a knock at the mission-home door. As I opened the door, the Fraser family stood before me. I invited them into the office and asked why they had driven the 250 miles to Toronto.

Brother Fraser replied, "We have come for our temple recommends. We are going to Salt Lake City to the temple of the Lord."

I said, "Brother Fraser, you don't even have a car. How will you make the trip?"

He then invited me to step outside to see the automobile he had purchased. My eyes fell upon a very old car. In Canada the winters are unusually hard on cars, causing extensive rusting. It appeared as though the winters had been more than harsh on the car that Brother Fraser had purchased.

I looked at the decrepit automobile and said to him, "This car will never get you to Salt Lake City."

Brother Fraser stood erect, his eyes blazing. Filled with faith, he then said to me, "President Monson, this car will get me and my family to the temple in Salt Lake City, and there is a difference."

I issued the temple recommends and bade them Godspeed on their journey westward.

Three weeks later they returned in the same car. I asked Brother Fraser to give me an account of his journey. He reported that the Lord had been with them throughout their visit to the Salt Lake Temple.

He said, "As we drove along the highway and the close of day would approach, we would inevitably pull into a filling station, there to refuel and to locate a place to stay for the night. The attendant would say, as he looked at our car, 'Where in the world are you going in this car?' After he heard our answer, he would say, 'I know some Mormons in our town. Perhaps they would like to visit with you.' In this way we found a place to stay and food to eat all the way to Salt Lake City and all the way back."

He continued, "No scene is of greater beauty than that which I experienced in the temple of God when my wife and I, kneeling at the altar, heard the door open and saw our children, dressed in white, come to our side. And how glorious it was to hear those words spoken that united us as an eternal family unit for time and all eternity."

His eyes glistened as he recounted the faith-promoting experience. I glanced out the front window at the old car. I knew within my heart that faith had carried the Fraser family to the temple of God and back to their home.

Tithing Pays

Very early one morning while I was serving as president of the Canadian Mission, I received a telephone call. As I answered the telephone, the person calling said to me, "Are you the president of the Mormon Church?"

"No," I replied.

She then said, "Are you president of the Mormon Church in Canada?"

"No."

Somewhat frustrated, she said, "Well, are you the man responsible for the two young men who come door-to-door with the message of Mormonism?"

I replied that I was, and she curtly stated, "Then get them off my back! We have had no peace in our home since these two young men called at our door. My foolish husband believes their message." She mentioned to me that her name was Rogers and gave me her address. I told her that I would respect her wish that the missionaries not call at their home, but that if Mr. Rogers wanted to continue his study of the truth, he could do so at our own residence on Lyndhurst Avenue.

I then felt impressed to say to her, "Mrs. Rogers, you're not able to accept the law of tithing, are you?"

She responded, "How did you know? How did you know?" She went on, "Why, of all the foolish doctrines, to think that those of us who can't get by on one hundred percent of our income could get by on nine-tenths. I can't buy that nonsense!" She then slammed the receiver in my ear.

As I returned to bed, Frances asked, "Who was that?"

"Some woman who doesn't want the missionaries," I replied.

I forgot about the incident. About two months later I was attending the fast and testimony meeting of the Toronto Branch, there to bless our newly arrived child, Clark Spencer Monson. The branch president said, "We have a number of ordinances today—some blessings, some confirmations. We would like now to invite the members of the Rogers family, seated on the front row, to each one be confirmed a member of the Church." Instantly the name Rogers flashed through my mind. I looked at the red-headed woman sitting on the front row. As I did so, I wondered, "Could this be the Mrs. Rogers who telephoned at two A.M.?" As though we were communicating one with another, Mrs. Rogers' eyes met mine, and she nodded her head affirmatively.

Following the ordinance work and the conclusion of the meeting, I went forward to congratulate the Rogers family. I said to her, "Could you possibly be the Mrs. Rogers who telephoned me early one morning?"

She said, "Yes, President Monson, and tithing pays."

I replied, "Tithing does pay, just as the missionaries have declared." I was happy to help confirm her a member of the Church.

Help in Naming Patriarchs

In 1964 I attended the quarterly conference of the Billings Stake in Montana with the specific assignment to name a patriarch. My visit with members of the stake presidency and my discussion with them concerning the names of possible candidates yielded no fruit. At the conclusion of the seven P.M. meeting, a patriarch was still not apparent. As I walked toward the rear of the chapel, I noticed the back of a man leaving the front door. Instantly I knew he was the patriarch. I said to the stake president, "Who is that brother?"

"That is Brother Davies, a member of our high council," he responded.

"President Anderson," I said, "he will be your patriarch." And thus Brother Davies became the patriarch of the Billings Stake. The Lord had called him. We needed simply to know the will of the Lord.

I once had an assignment to the Idaho Falls North Stake, there to name a patriarch. I reviewed the names of three illustrious men who were former leaders, yet I could not make a choice. Throughout Saturday I prayed earnestly for help, but no help came. At two o'clock Sunday morning I awakened, knowing that a patriarch's name had not been made known to me. I knelt down by the side of my bed and poured out my soul to the Lord and asked him for His divine help. As I returned to bed, I fell into a deep sleep. During my sleep, I dreamed a dream that eliminated two of the three brethren whom we had considered as a patriarch. As I awakened in the morning, I knew that the third individual was the patriarch whom the Lord wanted, and thus the call came to him to serve.

In 1971 I had the assignment to divide the Puget Sound

and the Tacoma stakes in Washington, thereby creating a third stake—the Mt. Rainier Stake. Naming the stake presidencies, the high councils, and so forth all fell into place. Remaining to be named was a patriarch for the Tacoma Stake. During the midst of my interview with a bishop concerning who would be appropriate members of the stake presidency, I felt compelled to ask him, "Who is the most spiritually minded man in the Tacoma Stake?"

"Walter Gehring," he responded without hesitation. This confirmed in my mind the thought I had had that Walter Gehring should be the patriarch. Suddenly the brother apologized for his statement and suggested that perhaps another brother or others were equally as spiritual. I told him that his first statement was the answer of confirmation I had needed. Thus Walter Gehring became a patriarch of the Tacoma Stake.

A few months later, I attended the quarterly conference of the Medford Stake in Oregon. Elder Gordon B. Hinckley was originally assigned to attend this conference, but an assignment to the East occasioned my substituting for him. It was necessary that a patriarch be named for this stake. The stake presidency had suggested several names. As I got off the plane at the Medford airport, I looked into the eyes of the stake clerk, who had come with the party to meet me. I knew immediately that he was to be the patriarch, though I said nothing to him nor to the others.

That afternoon, as we visited privately about the decision to be made and I asked each member of the stake presidency to submit to me the names of individuals who could meet the requirements I set forth that a patriarch should possess, the name of Douglas Shepherd, the stake clerk, was more prominently mentioned than any other. Brother Shepherd was ordained a patriarch on Sunday, April 18, 1971.

A Family Inspired by a Patriarch's Call

One evening in the winter month of January, I received a telephone call from my wife Frances's brother, Arnold Johnson. He was calling from New York City. He asked a question. I looked up the answer and gave him the details. He mentioned to me that he and his wife were in New York visiting their son, Reid, and attending an electrical engineers convention. I then pointed out that I would be in New York that weekend for a quarterly conference of the New York Stake. I invited Arnold and his wife, Janice, and the family to attend.

When I arrived in New York, I found that there was a need for a stake patriarch. The inspiration directed that Brother Paul Jespersen, a man whom I had released as president of the Chicago Stake when his business assignment took him to New York, was the man whom the Lord wanted to be a patriarch. It was then that I realized that Paul Jespersen had been the Scoutmaster of my brother-in-law, Arnold Johnson, in the old LeGrand Ward in Salt Lake City, and, according to Arnold, the man who had exerted a greater influence for good upon him than any other.

Then Arnold realized that Reid, his son, who was sitting by his side as a pillar of faith, a returned missionary from Sweden, had received his own name and blessing from Paul Jespersen when Paul lived in San Francisco. It was only natural that I should invite my family into the room as Paul Jespersen was ordained. Arnold bore testimony to him, even a testimony of gratitude, for the influence he'd had upon his life and upon his family. I noticed that, following these comments, Brother Jespersen's sons took a keener interest in the calling that had come to their father and embraced him in a spirit of gratitude.

I feel that our Heavenly Father brought to this glorious event, in sort of a family reunion, those who assembled. Arnold told me that this experience was one of the most faith-promoting he had ever had. I declared to him that it was no coincidence that he would be in the same setting where his former Scoutmaster was called to be a patriarch.

A Patriarch's Promise

❧

The late Percy K. Fetzer was one of the dearest friends I have ever had. He was a modern-day Paul, a fearless Peter, a guileless Nathanael. At the call of the Church, Brother Fetzer left his home, his business, and his family to nurture and care for our faithful Church members in the countries of Eastern Europe. He loved the people. He spoke the language of the heart. He had been ordained a patriarch to give blessings to worthy members in a host of nations.

During the long period of his service, Brother Fetzer made dozens of flights to Europe, blessing the members, instructing the priesthood, and providing an example of faith, of works, and of love.

While on an assignment in the land of Poland, he gave blessings to a number of German-speaking members who, due to the new geographical boundaries dictated by World War II, found themselves in a nation whose language they did not speak, isolated from the conferences of the Church. Upon his return to Salt Lake City, Brother Fetzer called me on the telephone and, with some anxiety, asked to come to my office. When he arrived, we embraced as old and dear friends do. I then asked him to explain his anxiety and concern.

Brother Fetzer related this account: "Brother Monson, I have just returned from Poland, where I gave patriarchal blessings to the Erich Konietz family." His voice wavered and tears began to course down his cheeks. He continued: "I try to live close to the Lord so that He will inspire the blessings I give. I have given blessings to the Konietz family that are impossible to fulfill. I have promised

Brother and Sister Konietz that, because of their faith, they will enter the temple of the Lord and have their entire family sealed to them for eternity as well as time. Brother Monson, they cannot leave their country. It is forbidden for them to do so. What have I done?"

I knew the heart and soul of Percy Fetzer. I responded, "If you made these promises as you did, let us now kneel down before God and ask for them to be fulfilled in His own time and in His own way."

As we prayed, a perfect peace filled our hearts. The matter was left with God. Several years later, and without fanfare or notice, there was announced a pact between the Federal Republic of Germany and Poland that allowed native Germans who had been trapped behind the Polish border following the war to emigrate to Germany. The Konietz family and most other member families in that land came home to their native Germany.

I had the privilege to ordain the father a bishop in the Dortmund Stake of the Church. The family then made that long-awaited trek to the temple in Switzerland. They dressed in clothing of spotless white. They knelt at a sacred altar to await that ordinance which binds father, mother, brothers, and sisters not only for time, but for all eternity. He who pronounced that sacred sealing ceremony was the temple president. More than this, however, he was the same servant of the Lord, Percy K. Fetzer, who, as a patriarch years before, had provided those precious promises in the patriarchal blessings he had bestowed.

Percy Fetzer and I both understood the expression: "The wisdom of God ofttimes appears as foolishness to men. But the greatest single lesson we can learn in mortality is that when God speaks and a man obeys, that man will always be right."

A Patriarch Nine Years Later

Many years back I was assigned to name a patriarch for a stake in Logan, Utah. I found such a man, wrote his name on a slip of paper, and placed the note inside my scriptures. My further review revealed that another worthy patriarch had moved to this same area, making unnecessary the naming of a new patriarch. None was named.

Nine years later I was again assigned a stake conference in Logan. Once more a patriarch was needed for the stake I was to visit. I had been using a new set of scriptures for several years and had them in my briefcase. However, as I prepared to leave my home for the drive to Logan, I took from the bookcase shelf an older set of scriptures, leaving the new ones at home.

During the conference I began my search for a patriarch: a worthy man, a blameless servant of God, one filled with faith, characterized by kindness. Pondering these requirements, I opened my scriptures and there discovered the slip of paper placed there long years before. I read the name written on the paper: Cecil B. Kenner. I asked the stake presidency if by chance Brother Kenner lived in this particular stake. I found he did. Cecil B. Kenner was that day ordained a patriarch.

A Pearl Diver's Gift

The gift of love is found throughout Polynesia: a love of God, a love of sacred things, and love for family, friends, and fellowmen.

Long years ago at Papeete, Tahiti, I met a distinguished yet humble man, extraordinarily blessed with the gift of love. He was eighty-four-year-old Tahauri Hutihuti from the island of Takaroa in the Tuamotu Island group. That evening I learned that he had been a faithful Church member all his life, and that he had longed for the day when there would be in the Pacific a holy temple of God. He had a love for the sacred ordinances he knew could be performed only in such a house. Patiently, and with purpose, he carefully saved his meager earnings as a pearl diver.

Then came the glorious news that a temple would be constructed in New Zealand. Brother Hutihuti prepared himself spiritually for that day. His wife did the same, as did the children. When the time came that the New Zealand Temple was to be dedicated, Tahauri reached beneath his bed and retrieved six hundred dollars—his life's savings accumulated throughout his forty years as a pearl diver—and gave all so that he might take his wife and his children to the temple of God in New Zealand.

As I said a tender good-bye to the Tahitians, each one came forward, placed an exquisite shell lei about my neck, and left an affectionate kiss upon my cheek. Tahauri, who did not speak English, stood by my side and spoke to me through an interpreter. The interpreter listened attentively and then, turning to me, reported: "Tahauri says he has no gift to bestow except the love of a full heart." Tahauri clasped my hand and kissed my cheek. Of all the gifts received that memorable night, the gift of this faithful man was the brightest.

A Mission to Complete

ॐ

A rather unique and frightening assignment came to me in the fall of 1965. Folkman D. Brown, then our director of Mormon relationships for the Boy Scouts of America, came to my office, having learned that I was about to depart for a lengthy assignment to visit the missions of New Zealand. He told me that his sister, Belva Jones, who had been stricken with terminal cancer, did not know how to break the sad news to her only son, a missionary in far-off New Zealand. Her wish, even her plea, was that he remain in the mission field and serve faithfully. She worried about his reaction, for the missionary, Elder Ryan Jones, had lost his father just a year earlier to the same dread disease.

I accepted the responsibility to inform Elder Jones of his mother's illness and to convey to him her wish that he remain in New Zealand until his service there was completed. After a missionary meeting held adjacent to the majestically beautiful New Zealand Temple, I met privately with Elder Jones and, as gently as I could, explained the situation of his mother. Naturally, there were tears—not all his—but then the handclasp of assurance and the pledge: "Tell my mother I shall serve, I shall pray, and I shall see her again."

I returned to Salt Lake City just in time to attend a conference of the Lost River Stake in Idaho. As I sat on the stand with the stake president, Burns Beal, my attention was drawn to the east side of the chapel, where the morning sunlight seemed to bathe an occupant of a front bench. President Beal told me the woman was Belva Jones. He said, "She has a missionary son in New Zealand. She is very ill and has requested a blessing."

Prior to that moment, I had not known where Belva Jones lived. My assignment that weekend could have been to any of many stakes. Yet the Lord, in His own way, had answered the prayer of faith of a devoted woman. Following the meeting, we had a most delightful visit together. I reported, word for word, the reaction and resolve of her son Ryan. A blessing was provided. A prayer was offered. A witness was received that Belva Jones would live to see Ryan again. This privilege she enjoyed. Just one month prior to her passing, Ryan returned, having successfully completed his mission.

I recognize that a Providence greater than chance sent me that day to this mother, with a personal message for her.

From Grand Junction to Düsseldorf

§

Some years ago I received the appointment to attend the Grand Junction Colorado Stake conference. As the plane circled the airport amid heavy snow, the pilot's voice announced that it appeared our landing would not be possible, and Grand Junction would of necessity be overflown. I knew that I had been assigned to this conference by a prophet, and prayed that the weather would permit a landing. Suddenly the pilot said, "There is an opening in the cloud cover. We'll attempt a landing." The word *attempt* is always a bit frightening to any air traveler.

Our landing was safely accomplished, and the entire conference went without incident. I wondered why I in particular had been assigned here. Before departing Grand Junction, the stake president asked if I would meet with a distraught mother and father whose son had announced his decision to leave his mission field after having just arrived there. When the conference throng had left, we knelt quietly in a private place—mother, father, stake president, and I. As I prayed in behalf of all, I could hear the muffled sobs of a sorrowing mother and disappointed father.

When we arose, the father said, "Brother Monson, do you really think our Heavenly Father can alter our son's announced decision to return home before completing his mission? Why is it that now when I am trying so hard to do what is right, my prayers are not heard?"

I responded, "Where is your son serving?"

He replied, "In Düsseldorf, Germany."

I placed my arm around mother and father and said to them, "Your prayers have been heard and are already being answered. With more than twenty-eight stake conferences being held this day attended by the General Authorities, I was assigned to your stake. Of all the General Authorities, I am the only one who has the assignment to meet with the missionaries in your son's mission in four days."

Their petition had been honored by the Lord. I was able to meet with their son. He responded to their pleadings. He remained and completed a highly successful mission.

Several years later I again visited the Grand Junction Colorado Stake. Again I met the same parents. Still the father had not qualified to have his large and beautiful family join mother and father in a sacred sealing ceremony, that this family might be a forever family. I suggested that if the family members would earnestly pray, they could qualify. I indicated that I would be pleased to officiate on that sacred occasion in the temple of God.

Mother pleaded, father strived, children urged, all prayed. Let me share with you a treasured letter that their young son, Todd, placed under his daddy's pillow on Father's Day morning:

> *Dad,*
>
> *I love you for what you are and not for what you aren't. Why don't you stop smoking? Millions of people have . . . why can't you? It's harmful to your health, to your lungs, your heart. If you can't keep the Word of Wisdom, you can't go to Heaven with me, Skip, Brad, Marc, Jeff, Jeannie, Pam, and their families. Us kids keep the Word of Wisdom. Why can't you? You are stronger and you are a man. Dad, I want to see you in heaven. We all do. We want to be a whole family in heaven . . . not half of one.*

*Dad, you and Mom ought to get two old bikes
and start riding around the park every night.
You are probably laughing right now, but I
wouldn't be. You laugh at those old people, jog-
ging around the park and riding bikes and walking, but they are going to outlive you. Because
they are exercising their lungs, their hearts, their
muscles. They are going to have the last laugh.*

*Come on, Dad, be a good guy—don't smoke,
drink, or anything else against our religion. We
want you at our graduation. If you do quit smoking and do good stuff like us, you and Mom can
go with Brother Monson and get married and
sealed to us in the temple. Come on, Dad—Mom
and us kids are just waiting for you. We want to
live with you forever. We love you. You're the
greatest, Dad.*

Love,
Todd

*P.S. And if the rest of us wrote one of these,
they'd say the same thing.*

*P.P.S. Mr. Newton has quit smoking. So can
you. You are closer to God than Mr. Newton!*

That plea, that prayer of faith, was heard and
answered. A night I shall ever treasure and long remember
was when this entire family assembled in a sacred room in
the Salt Lake Temple. Father was there; Mother was there;
every child was there. Ordinances eternal in their significance were performed. A humble prayer of gratitude
brought to a close this long-awaited evening.

Faith in Pago Pago

In October of 1965, President Hugh B. Brown, first counselor to President David O. McKay, and I were on assignment in the South Pacific. As we landed in Pago Pago, American Samoa, to hold a meeting, many members, including schoolchildren and their leaders, came out to meet us. They said, "We need your faith. We have no water. We have been fasting that with you would come moisture from heaven. If we don't have water soon, we will have to close the Mapusaga School and our chapels, because we are totally dependent upon rainfall for our water supply." It was apparent that the faith of these choice children of our Heavenly Father was great.

We met in the chapel prior to the meeting, and President Brown and I offered a prayer and asked our Heavenly Father to acknowledge the faith and fasting of the faithful Saints. As President Brown began to speak, we heard the clap of thunder, and the sky became dark. Then the rain descended. It fell so loudly against the metal roof that President Brown could scarcely be heard. With a smile he turned around to me and said, "Now that we've got it turned on, how do we turn it off?"

It rained for about two hours that morning, and the Saints rejoiced. They knew that their fasting had brought forth heaven's blessings.

Later at the airport, as we prepared for the short flight to Western Samoa, the pilot of the small plane said to the ground crew, "This is the most unusual weather pattern I have ever seen. Not a cloud is in the sky except over the Mormon school at Mapusaga. I don't understand it!"

President Brown said to me, "Here's your missionary opportunity. Go help him understand." I did so.

The Faith of a Child

·

Many years ago the Jack Methvin family lived about eighty miles from Shreveport, Louisiana. The family consisted of mother, father, several sons, and one daughter, Christal. By her very presence, Christal graced that home. She was but ten years old when death ended her earthly sojourn.

Christal liked to run and play on the spacious ranch where her family lived. She could ride horses skillfully and excelled in 4-H work, winning awards in the local and state fairs. Her future was bright, and life was wonderful. Then there was discovered on her leg an unusual lump. The specialists in New Orleans completed their diagnosis and rendered their verdict: carcinoma. The leg must be removed.

Christal recovered well from the surgery, lived as buoyantly as ever, and never complained. Then the doctors discovered that the cancer had spread to her tiny lungs. The Methvin family did not despair; rather, they planned a flight to Salt Lake City, where Christal could receive a blessing from one of the General Authorities. The Methvins knew none of the Brethren personally, so placing before Christal a picture of all the General Authorities, they asked her to make a selection. My name was selected.

Christal did not make the flight to Salt Lake City. Her condition deteriorated; the end drew nigh. But her faith did not waver. To her parents, she said, "Isn't stake conference approaching? Isn't a General Authority assigned? And why not Brother Monson? If I can't go to him, the Lord can send him to me."

Meanwhile in Salt Lake City, with no knowledge of the

events transpiring in Shreveport, a most unusual situation developed. For the weekend of the Shreveport Louisiana Stake conference, I had been assigned to El Paso, Texas. President Ezra Taft Benson called me to his office and explained that one of the other Brethren had done some preparatory work regarding the stake division in El Paso. He asked if I would mind were another to be assigned to El Paso and I assigned elsewhere. Of course there was no problem—anywhere would be fine with me. Then President Benson said, "Brother Monson, I feel impressed to have you visit the Shreveport Louisiana Stake." The assignment was accepted.

The day came. I arrived in Shreveport. Saturday afternoon was filled with meetings—one with the stake presidency, one with priesthood leaders, one with the patriarch, then yet another with the general leadership of the stake. Rather apologetically, the stake president asked if my schedule would permit me time to provide a blessing to a ten-year-old girl afflicted with cancer. Her name: Christal Methvin. I responded that, if possible, I would do so, and then inquired if she would be at the conference, or was she in a Shreveport hospital? Knowing the time was tightly scheduled, the president told me that Christal was confined to her home—more than eighty miles from Shreveport!

I examined the schedule of meetings for that evening and the next morning, even my return flight. There simply was no available time. An alternative suggestion came to mind. Could we not remember the little one in our public prayers at conference? Surely the Lord would understand. On this basis, we proceeded with the scheduled meetings.

When the word was communicated to the Methvin family, there was understanding but disappointment as well. Hadn't the Lord heard their prayers? Hadn't He provided that Brother Monson would come to Shreveport? Again the family prayed, asking for a final favor: that their precious Christal would realize her desire.

At the very moment the Methvin family knelt in prayer, the clock in the stake center showed the time to be 7:45 P.M. The leadership meeting had been inspirational. I was sorting my notes, preparing to step to the pulpit, when I heard a voice speak to my spirit. The message was brief, the words familiar: "Suffer the little children to come unto me, and forbid them not: for of such is the kingdom of God." (Mark 10:14.) My notes became a blur. My thoughts turned to a little girl in need of a blessing. The decision was made. The meeting schedule was altered. After all, people are more important than meetings. I turned to a bishop and asked that he leave the meeting and advise the Methvins.

The Methvin family had just arisen from their knees when the telephone rang and the message was relayed that early Sunday morning—the Lord's day—in a spirit of fasting and prayer, we would journey to Christal's bedside.

I shall ever remember that early-morning journey to a heaven the Methvin family called home. I have been in hallowed places—even holy houses—but never have I felt more strongly the presence of the Lord than in the Methvin home. Christal looked so tiny, lying on such a large bed. The room was bright and cheerful. The sunshine from the east window filled the bedroom with light as the Lord filled our hearts with love.

The family surrounded Christal's bedside. I gazed down at a child who was too ill to rise—almost too weak to speak. Her illness had now rendered her sightless. So strong was the spirit that I fell to my knees, took her frail hand in mine, and said simply, "Christal, I am here."

She parted her lips and whispered, "Brother Monson, I just knew you would come." I looked around the room. No one was standing. Each was on bended knee. A blessing was given. A faint smile crossed Christal's face. Her whispered "thank you" provided an appropriate benediction. Quietly, each filed from the room.

Four days later, on Thursday, as Church members in Shreveport joined their faith with the Methvin family and Christal's name was remembered in a special prayer to a kind and loving Heavenly Father, the pure spirit of Christal Methvin left its disease-ravaged body and entered the paradise of God.

The Child in the Balcony

§

At general conference in 1975, during the session when I was assigned to speak, my attention was drawn constantly to a little blond-haired girl seated on the first row in the balcony. That day I directed my remarks to my young friend in the balcony. I spoke of my experience with Christal Methvin, who was about her age.

Upon returning to my office, I found waiting for me this same young lady and also her grandmother. The young girl was Misti White from California. She said to me, "I have had a problem, Brother Monson, but not any longer. A person very dear to me told me to wait until I was eighteen to be baptized. My grandmother said I should be baptized now. I prayed for an answer and then said to Grandmother, 'Take me with you to conference. There Jesus will help me.'"

To conference they came, and so did divine help. Eagerly Misti took my hand and exclaimed, "You helped Him answer my prayer. Thank you."

Upon returning to California, Misti sent me a treasured letter, with this beautiful ending: "Brother Monson, I was baptized on November 29th. I am now very happy. Love, Misti." Faith does precede the miracle.

Distinct Impression

❧

One day, as I was walking in front of a Snelgrove ice cream store in Salt Lake City, a distinct impression came to me like the sound of a voice. I knew that I should pay a visit to the LDS Hospital, where Wayne Stucki, the teen-aged son of dear friends of mine, was a patient. He had been diagnosed as having a dread disease, and I realized that I was not to wait for my dinner or anything else I had scheduled that evening. So to the LDS Hospital I went and gave a blessing to Wayne Stucki.

I testify that our Heavenly Father responded to the faith of Wayne's mother and father and his family. Can you imagine my joy and the family's joy when Wayne began to recover from the operations he had had? He was called to serve as a missionary in Toronto, Canada, where I had once presided, to serve under President M. Russell Ballard. Upon his release, he returned home, married in the House of the Lord, and now has a lovely family of his own. I cherish that experience.

John's Race

❦

While on an assignment in Sweden, I was with a group of young people who shared with me an account of great courage that took place at a Scandinavian youth conference. It pertained to John Helander.

John was twenty-six years of age and was handicapped in that it was difficult for him to coordinate his motions. At a youth conference in Kungsbacka, Sweden, John took part in a 1500-meter race. He had no chance to win. More likely, he would be humiliated, mocked, derided, scorned. Perhaps John remembered another who had lived long ago and far away—even the Savior, Jesus Christ. Wasn't He mocked? Wasn't He derided? Wasn't He scorned? But He prevailed. He won His race. Maybe John could win his.

What a race it was! Struggling, surging, pressing, the runners bolted far beyond John. There was wonderment among the spectators. Who is this runner who lags so far behind? The participants on their second lap of this two-lap race passed John while he was but halfway through the first lap. Tension mounted as the runners pressed toward the tape. Who would win? Who would place second? Then came the final burst of speed; the tape was broken. The crowd cheered; the winner was proclaimed.

The race is over—or is it? Who is this contestant who continues to run when the race is ended? He now crosses the finish line on but his first lap. Doesn't the foolish lad know he has lost? Ever onward he struggles, the only participant now on the track. This is his race. This must be his victory. No one among the vast throng of spectators leaves. Every eye is on this valiant runner. He makes the final turn and moves toward the finish line. There is awe; there is admiration. Each spectator sees himself running his own race of life.

As John approaches the finish line, the audience, as one, rises to its feet. There is a loud applause of acclaim. Stumbling, falling, exhausted but victorious, John Helander breaks the newly tightened tape. (Officials are human beings too.) The cheering echoes for miles. And just maybe, if the ear is carefully attuned, that Great Scorekeeper—even the Lord—can be heard to say, "Well done, thou good and faithful servant." (Matthew 25:21.)

Faith in Tithing

Living in Debrecen, Hungary, was an aged member of the Church, Johann Denndorfer. Born of German parents, he, as a young man, went to Berlin in 1910 to seek work. There he not only found employment, but also, more significantly, he discovered the Church. Following World War I, he returned to Hungary and remained a lone voice for Mormonism during the next forty years.

During the time freedom was curtailed in Eastern Europe, Patriarch Walter Krause traveled from Germany to Hungary to pay a home teaching visit to Brother Denndorfer. He later reported to me that when he arrived and introduced himself, Brother Denndorfer said to him, "Before I shake the hand of a servant of the Lord, I first wish to pay my tithing." He then retrieved from a hiding place the tithing he had accumulated during the more-than-forty-year period. "Now I feel worthy to shake the hand of a servant of the Lord," he said.

Brother Krause gave Brother Denndorfer a patriarchal blessing, promising him that he would be able to go to the temple before he left mortality. Brother Denndorfer had applied many times before for permission to leave his country and journey to the temple in Switzerland, but had always been denied such permission. Now, with new hope and determination, Brother Denndorfer renewed his passport application. Miracle of miracles—it was approved!

Johann Denndorfer went to Switzerland. He received his own endowment in the temple at Zollikofen, his deceased wife was sealed to him, and he was able to do the work for a large number of his ancestors.

The word of the Lord provides a fitting tribute to the life of Johann Denndorfer and an appropriate benediction to these remarks: "For with God nothing shall be impossible." (Luke 1:37.)

Sunshine by the Elbe River

ॐ

On a gentle rise in the historic city of Freiberg, Germany, once a part of the German Democratic Republic, there stands a beautiful temple of God. The temple provides the eternal blessings of a loving Heavenly Father to His faithful Saints.

On Sunday morning, April 27, 1975, I stood on an outcropping of rock situated between the cities of Dresden and Meissen, high above the Elbe River, in the German Democratic Republic. I responded to the promptings of the Holy Spirit and offered a prayer of dedication on that land and its people. That prayer noted the faith of the members. It emphasized the tender feelings of many hearts filled with an overwhelming desire to obtain temple blessings. A plea for peace was expressed. Divine help was requested. I voiced the words: "Dear Father, let this be the beginning of a new day for the members of Thy church in this land."

Suddenly, from far below in the valley, a bell in a church steeple began to chime and the shrill crow of a rooster broke the morning silence, each heralding the commencement of a new day. Though my eyes were closed, I felt a warmth from the sun's rays reaching my face, my hands, my arms. How could this be? An incessant rain had been falling all morning. At the conclusion of the prayer, I gazed heavenward. I noted a ray of sunshine that penetrated an opening in the heavy clouds, a ray that engulfed the spot where our small group stood. From that moment I knew divine help was at hand.

In due time, with the enthusiastic approval of President Spencer W. Kimball and his counselors, a temple was proposed in this land situated behind the Berlin Wall. Full cooperation of government officials was forthcoming. A site was selected, plans were drawn, groundbreaking services were held, and construction commenced.

At the time of dedication, the attention of the international press was focused on this temple in its unusual setting. Words like "How?" and "Why?" were voiced frequently. This was particularly in evidence during the public open house when 89,872 persons visited the temple. At times the waiting period stretched to three hours, occasionally in the rain. None wavered. All were shown God's house.

During the dedicatory services, hymns of praise, testimonies of truth, tears of gratitude, and prayers of thanksgiving marked the historic event. To understand how, to comprehend why, it is necessary to know the faith, the devotion, the love of the members of the Church in that nation. Though there are fewer than five thousand in number, their activity levels exceeded those found anywhere else in the world.

During the many years I served on assignment in Eastern Europe, I noted the absence of spacious chapels with multiple teaching stations and grounds featuring the greenery of lawns and the blossoms of flowers. The meetinghouse libraries, as well as the personal libraries of our members, consisted only of the standard works, a hymnbook, and one or two other volumes. These books did not remain on bookcase shelves. Their teachings were engraved on the hearts of members. They were displayed in their daily lives. Service was a privilege. A branch president, forty-two years of age, had served in his calling for twenty-one years—half his life. Never was there a complaint—just gratitude.

In Leipzig, when the meetinghouse furnace failed one cold winter day, the meetings were not dismissed. Rather, the members met in the chill of the unheated building, sitting shoulder to shoulder, wearing their coats, singing the hymns of Zion and worshiping Him who counseled, "Be not weary in well doing" (2 Thessalonians 3:13); "Follow me" (Matthew 4:19); "Be thou humble; and the Lord thy God shall lead thee by the hand, and give thee answer to thy prayers" (D&C 112:10).

A Mother's Request

In early 1989 I received a letter from Martha Sharp of Wellsville, Utah, and read her entreaty seeking a blessing for her grown son, Steven, who was a patient at University Hospital in Salt Lake City. She described Steven's spiritual needs, as well as his physical needs, and indicated he likely would suffer the amputation of his foot. Her tears were felt in each word, and her feelings of love marked every sentence.

When I entered Steven's hospital room that night, I saw a man who just seemed built to ride a horse. Sensing this, I began to chat with him about a Western adventure film I had seen recently. I described the beautiful horses ridden by the principal characters. A warm smile came over Steven's face. Not until that moment did I note on his nightstand a book he had been reading. It was the book from which the film we had been discussing was made. Our conversation was warm and free from that point forward.

In describing his condition, Steven commented, "I hope they leave enough of my foot so that I can get it into a stirrup." I assured him we would remember him in our prayers. I told him that he had a wonderful mother who loved him and remembered him in his need, and a Heavenly Father who also loved and remembered him. Steven began to weep. A special spirit filled the room. A blessing was given, a heart cleansed, a memory of home and family rekindled, and a mother comforted.

Temple Pictures

ૹ

When I first visited Czechoslovakia, accompanied by Hans B. Ringger, regional representative, long before the freedom bell sounded, I was met by Jiri Snederfler, our leader through this dark period, and Olga Snederfler, his wife. I went to their home in Prague, where the branch met. Displayed on the walls of the room in which we assembled were picture after picture of the Salt Lake Temple. I said to Sister Snederfler, "Your husband must truly love the temple."

She responded, "I too. I too."

We sat down for some soup Sister Snederfler had prepared, after which she brought out a treasure trove: an album containing individual pictures of the missionaries who were serving there in 1950 when the government edict came for the mission to be closed. As she slowly leafed through the pictures of different missionaries, she would say, "Wonderful boy. Wonderful boy."

Brother Snederfler had been a courageous Church leader in Czechoslovakia and had been willing to put everything on the line for the gospel. When the opportunity came that we would seek recognition for the Church in that country, the government leaders, then Communist, said, "Don't send an American. Don't send a German. Don't send a Swiss. Send a citizen of Czechoslovakia."

There were ominous implications in that particular statement, because to have admitted that you were a church leader during this period of the prohibition of religion could mean imprisonment. And yet this call came to Brother Snederfler to be the designated person to go before the government and to state forthrightly that he was the leader of The Church of Jesus Christ of Latter-day Saints for all of Czechoslovakia and that he was seeking recognition for his church. He later told me that he had been somewhat frightened and had asked for the prayers of his brothers and sisters in the Prague Branch. He went to his sweet wife, Olga, and said to her, "I love you. I don't know when, or if, I'll be back; but I love the gospel, and I must follow my Savior. Pray for me."

With that spirit of faith and devotion, Brother Snederfler went before the government officials and acknowledged that he was the leader of the Church and that he was there to seek a restoration of the recognition the Church had enjoyed long years before.

In the meantime, Elder Russell M. Nelson had been working tirelessly to bring about the desired decision. Later Brother Snederfler heard the good news: "Your church is again recognized in Czechoslovakia." How eager Brother Snederfler was to tell his dear wife and the other stalwart members of the Church the wonderful news that once again missionaries could come to Czechoslovakia and the Church could provide a haven for freedom of worship in that nation. It was a happy day for Czechoslovakia.

In 1991 Jiri and Olga Snederfler responded to their calls to serve as temple president and matron of the Freiberg Germany Temple, which faithful members of the Church in Germany, Czechoslovakia, and surrounding nations attend. These two saintly souls found themselves each day in the Lord's house they so dearly loved.

PRAYER AVAILETH MUCH

*The prayers of the faithful
shall be heard.*

2 NEPHI 26:15

Emergency Decision

Just prior to my eighteenth birthday, with the United States still engaged in fighting World War II, I had to make a decision regarding what branch of military service I was going to enter.

At the Federal Building in Salt Lake City, where we were to be sworn in, forty-two young men stood fearful and in wonderment concerning the future. A number of parents likewise stood by our sides, including my father.

Two chief petty officers said, "You men have to make a choice. You may join the regular Navy for a four-year period. You will no doubt receive schooling and extra preferences, because the Navy will have an investment in you. Or you may elect to join the Naval Reserve, which is a period of obligation for the duration of the war and six months. The Navy will not be as kind to you if you join the Reserve."

Forty chose the regular Navy; one could not pass the physical examination. I alone remained to choose. I turned to my father and asked him, "Dad, what shall I do?"

With tears in his eyes and emotion in his voice, he said, "I don't know."

I then sent a prayer heavenward to my Heavenly Father and asked for counsel. The reply came not in the form of an answer, but rather in the form of a question. I asked the chief petty officer, "When you had the choice to make, how did you choose?"

With a look of obvious embarrassment he said, "I joined the Naval Reserve."

I asked the same question of the second petty officer and received the same answer.

I then said to the two of them, "You men are men of experience and judgment. I'll follow your example—I'll take the Naval Reserve."

Shortly thereafter the war ended, and within a year my service had been completed, and I was back at the University of Utah. Who knows what my future might have been had I not paused to pray in this moment of my life.

Marriage Formula

❧

My wife, Frances, and I were married in the Salt Lake Temple. He who performed the ceremony, Benjamin Bowring, counseled us: "May I offer you newlyweds a formula that will insure that any disagreement you may have will last no longer than one day? Every night kneel by the side of your bed. One night, Brother Monson, you offer the prayer, aloud, on bended knee. The next night you, Sister Monson, offer the prayer, aloud, on bended knee. I can then assure you that any misunderstanding that develops during the day will vanish as you pray. You simply can't pray together and retain any but the best of feelings toward one another."

When I was called to the Council of the Twelve in 1963, President McKay asked me concerning my family. I related to him this guiding formula of prayer and bore witness to its validity. He sat back in his large leather chair and, with a smile, responded, "The same formula that has worked for you has blessed the lives of my family during all the years of our marriage."

Prayer is the passport to spiritual power.

Nursery Rhyme Prayer

When our oldest son was about three, he would kneel with his mother and me in our evening prayer. I was serving as the bishop of the ward at the time, and a lovely lady in the ward, Margaret Lister, lay perilously ill with cancer. Each night we would pray for Sister Lister.

One evening our tiny son offered the prayer and confused the words of the prayer with a story from a nursery book. He began: "Heavenly Father, please bless Sister Lister, Henny Penny, Chicken Licken, Turkey Lurkey, and all the little folks." We held back the smiles that evening.

Later we were humbled as Margaret Lister sustained a complete recovery. We do not demean the prayer of a child. After all, our children have more recently been with our Heavenly Father than have we.

Hidden Blessing

While I was serving as the bishop of the Sixth-Seventh Ward, my counselors and I pondered the need for a YMMIA superintendent. One evening we went through a list of names but could receive no answer as to whom it should be. We prayed for inspiration.

The next day I was riding south on Main Street on a Salt Lake City Lines bus, pondering the problem pertaining to our MIA. I felt the impression to look out the west window of the bus, and there I saw, walking up the street, a former member of our ward. His name was Jack Reed. Instantly I knew he was to be the MIA superintendent. I thought to myself, "If only he lived in our ward."

That night as we met in council, I related to my counselors this experience. My first counselor, Joseph M. Cox, smiled and said, "Tom, did you know that Jack Reed has moved back within our ward?"

I replied, "I did not know, but the Lord does know."

We went to Brother Reed's father's home, where Jack was living, and said to him, "Jack, the Lord wants you to serve in the MIA as superintendent. Will you respond?"

He pointed out that his experience had all been in the Sunday School; but then he said, "If the Lord wants me to serve, I'm ready."

He became one of the finest MIA superintendents our ward ever had. Furthermore, during the performance of his official duties, he met and married the age group counselor of the stake YWMIA, a lovely woman by the name of Evelyn Dame. They were married in the House of the Lord.

MIA brought them together. A call to serve had prepared the opportunity.

A Bishop's Prayers

Every bishop needs a sacred grove to which he can retire to meditate and to pray for guidance. Mine was our old ward chapel. I could not begin to count the occasions when on a dark night at a late hour I would make my way to the stand of that building where I had been blessed, confirmed, ordained, taught, and eventually called to preside. The chapel was dimly lighted by the street light in front; not a sound would be heard, no intruder to disturb. I would kneel and share with Him above my thoughts, my concerns, my problems.

On one occasion, a year of drought, the commodities at the storehouse had not been their usual quality, nor had they been found in abundance. Many products were missing, especially fresh fruit. My prayer that night is sacred to me. I pleaded that the widows in my ward were the finest women I knew in mortality, that their needs were simple and conservative, that they had no resources on which they might rely. Could not some way be found for them to receive the fruit that they needed for well-balanced meals?

The next morning I received a call from a ward member, the proprietor of a produce business. "Bishop," he said, "I would like to send a semitrailer filled with oranges, grapefruit, and bananas to the bishops' storehouse to be given to those in need. Could you make arrangements?" Could I make arrangements! The storehouse was alerted. Then each bishop was telephoned and the entire shipment distributed. Bishop Jesse M. Drury, that beloved welfare pioneer and storekeeper, said he had never witnessed a day like it before. He described the occasion with one word: "Wonderful!"

A Mother's Prayer Answered

&

In 1951, as bishop of the Sixth-Seventh Ward, I received an assignment from our stake president to supply the stake with the names of two possible stake missionaries. My counselors and I prayed about the selection and then reviewed the listing of priesthood bearers within the ward.

We had a card file in which each individual card contained the name of the head of the family. One at a time, we eliminated the name of each of the high priests and each of the elders. My comment would be, "We can't recommend him; he's our Scoutmaster," or "We would be foolish to recommend him; he's busy teaching the priests quorum."

Finally, we commenced the file of the seventy. I came to a card that contained the name of Richard W. Moon and said to my counselors, "We sure won't recommend him. He's the finest assistant Sunday School superintendent we've ever had." I then attempted to put the card face down on the stack, but the card would not leave my thumb and index finger. It was as though it were glued to them. I tugged at the card, but still it would not come loose. I then said to my counselors, "The Lord needs Richard W. Moon as a stake missionary more than we need him as an assistant Sunday School superintendent."

I called the stake president, President Stewart, and related the experience. He said, "Brother Monson, under the circumstances, go immediately to Brother Moon's home and extend to him a call to serve."

We adjourned our meeting and went to Richard Moon's home, only to find no one there. A neighbor said that he was visiting his mother's home, which also was situated within our ward. So we went to the home of Art and Isabel Moon. Isabel, Richard's mother, opened the door to us and invited us in. I said that we had come to visit with Richard about a mission. I then told her the circumstances. Tears welled up in her eyes, and she said, "Bishop, ever since we received your announcement that the Church was looking for seventies who could fill missions, I have prayed that my son might be appointed. I wondered how, with his wife and tiny children, he could be a full-time missionary. Not once did I think of a stake mission. Your visit is in answer to my prayer."

Richard W. Moon became a most successful stake missionary. He served as a district president and brought a number of people into the Church. He then returned to the ward a better assistant Sunday School superintendent than he ever would have been, had he not had his mission experience.

A Last Request

&

Many years ago I stood by the bedside of a young man, the father of two children, as he hovered between life and the great beyond. He took my hand in his, looked into my eyes, and pleaded, "Bishop, I know I am about to die. Tell me what happens to my spirit when I die."

I prayed for heavenly guidance before attempting to respond. My attention was directed to the Book of Mormon, which rested on the table beside his bed. I held the book in my hand, and that book opened to the fortieth chapter of Alma. I began to read aloud:

"Now my son, here is somewhat more I would say unto thee; for I perceive that thy mind is worried concerning the resurrection of the dead. . . .

"Now, concerning the state of the soul between death and the resurrection—Behold, it has been made known unto me by an angel, that the spirits of all men, as soon as they are departed from this mortal body, . . . are taken home to that God who gave them life.

"And then shall it come to pass, that the spirits of those who are righteous are received into a state of happiness, which is called paradise, a state of rest, a state of peace, where they shall rest from all their troubles and from all care, and sorrow." (Alma 40:1, 11-12.)

My young friend, through moist eyes and with an expression of profound gratitude, whispered a silent but eloquent "Thank you."

Children's Prayers in Sauniatu

In February 1965, on my first visit to the fabled village of Sauniatu, Samoa, so loved by President David O. McKay, my wife and I met with a large gathering of small children. At the conclusion of our messages to these shy but beautiful youngsters, I suggested to the native Samoan teacher that we go forward with the closing exercises. As he announced the final hymn, the distinct impression came to me that I should personally greet each of these children. My watch revealed that the time was too short for such a privilege, so I discounted the impression.

Before the benediction was to be spoken, I again felt this strong impression to shake the hand of each child. This time I made the desire known to the instructor, who displayed a broad and beautiful smile. He spoke in Samoan to the children, and they beamed their approval of his comments.

The instructor then revealed to me the reason for his and their joy. He said, "When we learned that President McKay had assigned a member of the Council of the Twelve to visit us in faraway Samoa, I told the children if they would each one earnestly and sincerely pray and exert faith like the Bible accounts of old, that the apostle would visit our tiny village at Sauniatu, and, through their faith, he would be impressed to greet each child with a personal handclasp."

Tears could not be restrained as each of those precious boys and girls walked shyly by and whispered softly to us a sweet *talofa lava*. The gift of faith had been evidenced.

Extra Copies

While attending the annual meetings of the Boy Scouts of America in 1971, I took with me several copies of the *New Era*, that I might share with officials of Scouting this excellent publication. As I opened the package, I found that my secretary, for no accountable reason, had given me two extra copies of the June issue, an issue that featured temple marriage. I left the two copies in the hotel room and, as planned, distributed the other copies.

On the final day of the conference, I had no desire to attend the scheduled luncheon but felt compelled to return to my room. The telephone was ringing as I entered. The caller introduced herself as Sister Knotts. She asked if I could provide a blessing for her ten-year-old daughter. I agreed readily, and she indicated that she and her husband, their daughter, and their son would come immediately to my hotel room. As I waited, I prayed for help. The applause of the convention was replaced by the peace of prayer.

Then came the knock at the door and the privilege of meeting a choice Latter-day Saint family. Ten-year-old Deanna walked with the aid of crutches. Cancer had required the amputation of her left leg. Her clothing was clean, her countenance radiant, her trust in God unwavering. A blessing was provided. Mother and son knelt by the side of the bed, while the father and I placed our hands on tiny Deanna. We were directed by the Spirit of God. We were humbled by its power.

I felt the tears course down my cheeks and tumble upon my hands as they rested on the head of that beautiful

child of God. I spoke of eternal ordinances and family exal-
tation. The Lord prompted me to urge this family to enter
the holy temple of God. At the conclusion of the blessing, I
learned that such a temple visit was planned for that very
summer. Questions pertaining to the temple were asked. I
heard no heavenly voice, nor did I see a vision. Yet there
came to me a certain statement: "Refer to the *New Era*." I
looked to the dresser, and there were the two copies of the
temple issue of the *New Era*. One was given to Deanna. One
was provided her parents. Each was reviewed and read.

The Knotts family said farewell, and once again the
room was still. A prayer of gratitude came easily and, once
more, the resolve to provide a place for prayer.

Prayers in Poland

ॐ

Poland has had more wars fought on its soil than any other nation in the world. There is now a glorious mission there. Elder Russell M. Nelson, Elder Hans Ringger, and I were there a few years ago when Poland was behind the Iron Curtain, to seek permission for more missionaries to be in Poland. We had just one couple there at the time—one couple for an entire nation. The first couple who served in Warsaw, Poland, were tremendous people from Chicago, Brother and Sister Mazur.

On the day when Elder Nelson, Elder Ringger, and I were in Poland, we were in the company of another wonderful couple by the name of Juliusz and Dorothy Fussek. I had known Brother Fussek when he operated a stitcher-trimmer machine at the Church Printing Services. He and his wife went on their mission to Poland assuming it would be for eighteen months. They actually served close to five years. While in Poland, they lived in a little hovel with just a tiny shower, and they endured the privation there for the entire period. However, the Lord utilized them in a mighty manner to bring about a miracle. When Brother Nelson and Brother Ringger and I, accompanied by Elder Fussek, met with Minister Adam Wopatka of the Polish Ministry of Religion, he said, "Your church is welcome here. You may build your buildings, you may send your missionaries. You are welcome in Poland. This man," pointing to Juliusz Fussek, "and his wife have served your church well. You can be grateful for their example and their work, as well as that of their predecessors."

As we left the ministry and went to our hotel rooms, we

got down upon our knees and thanked our Heavenly Father for the manner in which He had responded to the prayers of faith that the doors of nations might be opened so that the gospel of Jesus Christ might be proclaimed. We thanked Him also for the faithful and dedicated service of Elder and Sister Fussek and Elder and Sister Mazur.

MISSIONARY MOMENTS

*How beautiful are the feet of them
that preach the gospel of peace,
and bring glad tidings of good things!*

ROMANS 10:15

An Elder's Influence on His Father

In 1987 the Salt Lake City newspapers carried an obituary notice for Fred Sudbury. It indicated that he was survived by his wife, Pearl, and a son, Craig; that he was a member of The Church of Jesus Christ of Latter-day Saints; and that his marriage had been solemnized in the Salt Lake Temple. What the obituary notice could not adequately convey was the inspiring human drama that preceded Fred's passing.

Some years before, Craig Sudbury and his parents had come to my office prior to Craig's departure for the Australia Melbourne Mission. Twenty-three years earlier, Craig's mother had married Fred, who was proud of his family but did not share their love for the Church and, indeed, was not a member.

In a conversation with Craig, he confided to me his deep and abiding love for his parents and his hope that somehow, in some way, his father would be touched by the Spirit and open his heart to the gospel of Jesus Christ. I prayed for inspiration concerning how such a desire might be fulfilled. Such inspiration came, and I said to Craig, "Serve the Lord with all your heart. Be obedient to your sacred calling. Each week write a letter to your parents, and on occasion, write to Dad personally. Let him know that you love him, and tell him why you're grateful to be his son." He thanked me.

About eighteen months later, Pearl came to the office and, in sentences punctuated by tears, said to me, "It has been almost two years since Craig departed for his mission. He has never failed in writing a letter to us each week.

Recently, my husband, Fred, stood for the first time in a testimony meeting and said, 'All of you know that I am not a member of the Church, but something has happened to me since Craig left for his mission. His letters have touched my soul. May I share one with you?

> *Dear Dad,*
>
> *Today we taught a choice family about the plan of salvation and blessings of exaltation in the celestial kingdom. I thought of our family. More than anything in the world I want to be with you and Mother in the celestial kingdom. For me it just wouldn't be a celestial kingdom if you were not there. I'm grateful to be your son, Dad, and want you to know that I love you.*
>
> > *Your missionary son,*
> > *Craig*

"'Pearl doesn't know what I plan to say. After twenty-six years of marriage, I have made my decision to become a member of the Church, for I know the gospel message is the word of God. My son's mission has moved me to action. I have made arrangements for my wife and me to meet Craig when he completes his mission. I will be his final baptism as a full-time missionary of the Lord.'" He heard the message, he saw the light, he embraced the truth.

A young missionary with unwavering faith had participated with God in a modern-day miracle. His challenge to communicate with one whom he loved had been made more difficult by the barrier of the thousands of miles that lay between him and home. But the spirit of love spanned the vast expanse of the blue Pacific, and heart spoke to heart in divine dialogue.

No missionary stood so tall as did Craig Sudbury when, in far-off Australia, he helped his father into water waist-deep and, raising his right arm to the square, repeated those sacred words: "Fred Sudbury, having been commissioned of Jesus Christ, I baptize you in the name of the Father, and of the Son, and of the Holy Ghost."

The prayer of a mother, the faith of a father, the service of a son brought forth the miracle of God.

Seven Years Plus Two

When my grandfather Nels Monson was a boy, his family lived in Sweden. They joined the Church there, then took a ship to America. On the way, the ship dropped anchor at Liverpool and picked up some families from England, Scotland, and Ireland. During the long voyage over, my grandfather met and fell in love with a sweet little English girl. He waited seven years so that she could grow up and marry him.

The first entry in his missionary journal expressed eloquently his gratitude: "Today, in the Salt Lake Temple, Maria Mace became my eternal wife." The entry written three days later was more somber: "Tonight the bishop came to our house. I have been called to serve a two-year mission to Scandinavia. My dear wife will remain at home and sustain me." I treasure such faith. I cherish such commitment.

Years later, as a member of the Twelve, I was reading Nels Monson's journal to my wife, Frances, when we were on an assignment in Sweden. We discovered that during his mission he had been in her grandfather's home. The journal entry that I treasure most is one where my grandfather reported visiting the family of my wife's grandfather—the Johnson family—in Dalarna to receive the family's tithing, and he recorded the family members by name. Later we looked in the windows of that old farmhouse. Imagine the two of us looking in the windows of a farmhouse where our grandfathers prayed together and studied together and ate together.

An Elder's Faith

%

Shortly after my call to the Council of the Twelve, one of my assignments was to direct missionary labors in the missions of the West Coast of North America.

I held a meeting one day in San Mateo, California, and as I listened to the testimonies of the missionaries, I noted that one elder had a terribly scarred face. The mission president, Howard Allen, advised me that Elder Nichols had been thrown through the windshield of his automobile in a terrible accident just a few months earlier. He then pointed out that Elder Nichols' parents were nonmembers and were threatening to sue the Church due to the injury. Doctors had despaired of the boy ever again regaining a pleasing appearance and felt that plastic surgery could do but little in his particular case.

I felt the strong impression to give to Elder Nichols a blessing. President Allen and I took him aside and gave him such a blessing. The spirit was surely present.

In the fall of 1969 my wife, Frances, and I were looking at carpeting in a store in Salt Lake City. The young man handling the carpet came forward and asked if I remembered him. I told him that he looked vaguely familiar, but that I couldn't quite place his name. He then stepped over and sat behind a lamp so that the light of the lamp cast its brilliance upon his face. He said, "Look closely at my face and then see if you can remember."

As I examined his face, I noted thin, scarcely discernable scars running across his nose, forehead, and cheeks. It was then that I realized this was Elder Nichols, the horribly scarred boy who had received a blessing in San Mateo while serving as a missionary in the Northern California Mission.

When I identified him, he smilingly said, "Brother Monson, even the plastic surgeons have called my case a miracle. I told them it was the intervention of Divine Providence through a priesthood blessing coupled with faith."

Elder Nichols was among the most handsome of young men.

A Missionary's Telegram

Many years ago I was called and sustained at a young age to preside in a large ward in Salt Lake City. One prominent couple with a son in the mission field became bitter in their hearts through frustrated position seeking. A vow was made by them to never darken the door of the chapel again. For a long time they kept their vow. The weeks turned to months, and the months approached a year. The bitterness had deepened, the resolve hardened.

One Sunday evening we planned to hear from a returning missionary who had been a friend to the son of our embittered couple. I remember how my heart yearned for this fine couple to return to activity. I had explored my every avenue of hope—personal visits, personal pleadings, personal prayer. This particular Sunday at four P.M. I retired to a private place and poured out my feelings to my Heavenly Father. As I arose from my knees, I felt a peace beyond description fill my soul. I knew that this couple would attend sacrament meeting that very evening.

The appointed hour approached; there was no sign of the couple. My counselors went to the stand. My watch showed but two minutes remaining. I peered out the window in the entranceway toward the street where the family lived. Just then their green Buick approached the ward, and they made their way to the chapel. With hesitation they came up the stairway. I greeted them: "Welcome home. We've missed you. We need you." The mother handed me a telegram that read: "Be at church this Sunday. I know you won't let me down. /s/ Your missionary son, Jack." I noted the time of the telegram—four P.M., the exact time I had been upon my knees. They were again active from that day forth.

A Mother's Hands

❧

When I was president of the Canadian Mission, the family of one noble missionary son lived in the harsh climate of Star Valley, Wyoming. Summer there is brief and warm, while winter is long and cold. When a fine son of nineteen said farewell to home and family, he knew on whom the burden of work would fall. Father was ill and limited. To mother came the task of milking by hand the small dairy herd that sustained the family.

During the time of my service in Canada, I attended a seminar for all mission presidents held in Salt Lake City. My wife and I were privileged to devote an evening to meeting the parents of those missionaries who served with us. Some parents were wealthy and handsomely attired, while others were less affluent, of modest means and rather shy; but all were proud of their special missionary and prayed and sacrificed for his welfare.

Of all the parents whom I met that evening, the best remembered was that mother from Star Valley. As she took my hand in hers, I felt the large cal"uses that revealed the manual labor she daily performed. Almost apologetically, she attempted to excuse her rough hands, her wind-whipped face. She whispered, "Tell our son Spencer that we love him, that we're proud of him, and that we pray daily for him."

She, who with that same hand clasped in the hand of God had walked bravely into the valley of the shadow of death to bring to this mortal life her son, had indelibly impressed my life. A mother's labor had sanctified a son's service.

A Prayer in Sudbury

In the Canadian Mission during the year 1960, I assigned Elder Clinton Buttars to the nickel-mining city of Sudbury, Ontario. The landscape was bleak, the missionary opportunities somewhat limited, and yet Clinton Buttars and his companion commenced to proselyte in one of the more affluent areas of the community.

They called at the home of Morley Dimma but found that he was at work and had his evenings fully occupied, as reported by his wife. Mrs. Dimma then suggested that the missionaries might wish to call upon him at his office. They grasped the opportunity and went to the office suite occupied by Mr. Dimma, who was the local agent of a large insurance firm.

As they were escorted into his inner office and Mr. Dimma asked them the nature of their visit, fear engulfed them. Suddenly Elder Buttars asked the question, "Mr. Dimma, how long has it been since you prayed?"

Mr. Dimma replied jokingly, "I haven't prayed since I was at my mother's knee."

Elder Buttars then said, "Would you join us in prayer?" He dropped to his knees, for there was no place else to go. His companion followed his lead, and reluctantly Mr. Dimma likewise joined in an attitude of prayer—the first time, as he stated, since he was at his mother's knee.

Concluding the prayer, the two missionaries and Mr. Dimma rose to their feet. Mr. Dimma then reported to them that he felt a strangeness come over him during that prayer and a desire to listen to the message that the missionaries had brought.

Mr. Dimma, his wife, and their children were converted

to the Church. He was so thrilled with the truth he had discovered in the gospel of Jesus Christ that he asked if he might extend a personal invitation to the several hundred members of his former religious congregation to each hear the message in his home. Four other missionaries were dispatched to the Sudbury area to accommodate this request.

A thriving branch and a lovely building later characterized the position of the Church in Sudbury, Ontario.

Testimony on a Bus

Some years ago I worked with Sharman Hummel in the printing business in Salt Lake City. I once gave him a ride home from work and asked him how he came to receive his testimony of the gospel. He responded, "It's interesting, Tom, that you asked me that question, for this very week my wife, my children, and I are going to the Manti Temple to be sealed for all eternity."

He continued his account: "We lived in the East. I was journeying by bus to San Francisco to establish myself in a new printing company, and then I was going to send for my wife and children. All the way from New York City to Salt Lake City, the bus trip was uneventful. But in Salt Lake City there entered the bus a little girl who sat next to me. As we journeyed westward, I noticed a road sign that read 'Visit the Mormon Sunday School this week.' I said to the little girl, 'I guess there are a lot of Mormons in Utah, aren't there?'

"She replied, 'Yes, sir.'

"Then I said to her, 'Are you a Mormon?'

"Again, 'Yes, sir.'

"'What do Mormons believe?'"

The girl recited the first Article of Faith, and then she talked about it. Continuing, she gave him the second Article of Faith and talked about it. Then she gave him the third, and the fourth, and the fifth, and the sixth, and all of the Articles of Faith and talked about all of them. She knew them consecutively.

Sharman Hummel said, "By the time she arrived at her destination, I was profoundly impressed. All the way to

San Francisco I thought, 'What is it that prompts that young girl to know her doctrine so well?'

"When I arrived in San Francisco, the very first thing I did was to look through the yellow pages for The Church of Jesus Christ of Latter-day Saints. I called the mission president, J. Leonard Love, and he sent two missionaries to where I was staying. I became a member of the Church, my wife became a member, all of our children became members, in part because a young girl knew her Articles of Faith."

As my friend told me this story, I thought of the words of the Apostle Paul: "For I am not ashamed of the gospel of Christ: for it is the power of God unto salvation." (Romans 1:16.)

Then Sharman said, "I have but one regret. I never asked for her name. I've never been able to properly thank her."

Several years later I was in Milwaukee, Wisconsin, dedicating the Milwaukee Stake Center. On the front row I noticed the Hummel family. As I greeted them, I found that they had moved to Milwaukee, Sharman having found a better position there. I asked concerning his current status in the Church. He replied, "I am a president in the seventies quorum and a stake missionary."

I then said, "How many people have you brought to a knowledge of the truth?"

"Twenty-four," he replied.

I thought to myself, "All because a young girl knew her Articles of Faith and had the ability and the courage to proclaim the truth to one who was seeking the light of the gospel."

A Hospital Fast

&

When I was a mission president, we had one young missionary who was very ill. After the missionary had been in the hospital for several weeks, the doctor prepared to undertake extremely serious and complicated surgery and he asked that we send for the missionary's mother and father. He advised there was a possibility the patient would not survive the surgery.

The parents came. Late one evening, the father and I entered a hospital room in Toronto, Canada, placed our hands upon the head of the young missionary, and gave him a blessing. What happened following that blessing was a testimony to me.

The missionary was in a six-bed ward in the hospital. The other five beds were occupied by men with a variety of illnesses. The morning of the missionary's surgery, his bed was empty. The nurse came into the room with the breakfast the five men normally ate. She took a tray over to the patient in bed number one and said, "Fried eggs this morning, and I have an extra portion for you."

The occupant of bed number one had suffered an accident with his lawn mower. Other than an injured toe, he was well physically. He said to the nurse, "I'll not be eating this morning."

"All right, we shall give your breakfast to your partner in bed number two."

As she approached that patient, he said, "I think I'll not eat this morning."

Each of the five men declined breakfast.

The nurse exclaimed, "Every other morning you eat us

out of house and home, and today not one of you wants to eat! What is the reason?"

Then the man who occupied bed number six answered: "You see, bed number three is empty. Our friend is in the operating room under the surgeon's hands. He needs all the help he can get. He is a missionary for his church, and while we have been patients in this ward, he has talked to us about the principles of his church—principles of prayer, of faith, of fasting wherein we call upon the Lord for blessings." He continued, "We don't know much about the Mormon church, but we have learned a great deal about our friend, and we are fasting for him today."

The operation was a success. When I attempted to pay the doctor, he countered, "Why, it would be dishonest for me to accept a fee. I have never before performed surgery when my hands seemed to be guided by a power that was other than my own. No," he said, "I wouldn't take a fee for the surgery that Someone on high helped me to perform."

After a few months of recuperation at home, the missionary returned to Toronto and completed his missionary labors.

The Cornwall Newspaper

❧

At a missionary conference in Canada, I handed to each pair of missionaries a typewritten presentation that could well be utilized in obtaining newspaper publicity. A request was made that missionaries take the article in type-written form and submit it to the newspapers in their areas of labor rather than reverting to the practice of an interview.

Elder Michael Erdman and his companion debated whether it would be worthwhile to take the prepared article to the newspaper in Cornwall, Ontario, for Cornwall was always a particularly difficult city for the missionaries of the Canadian Mission. Finally Elder Erdman said, "If the president of the mission has asked us to do so, let us go forward and comply." This they did, and a fine article appeared on the front page of the second section of the daily newspaper.

Prior to this day, and unbeknown to us, the Ministerial Association of Cornwall had banded together and spread a vicious rumor that the Mormons were not Christians and therefore the swimming pool of the YMCA, our only baptism facility, should be closed to use by Mormons. The night our newspaper article appeared was the night when the board of trustees of the YMCA was to make its decision regarding our use of the pool.

The chairman of the YMCA board read the article submitted by the missionaries and was impressed by its content. The headline, "Mormons Are Truly Christians," answered the question he had within his heart. That night he read the article to the assembled board, and the petition of the Ministerial Association was soundly rejected. Furthermore, the YMCA pool, which, prior to this time, had been rented to us at twenty dollars per use, was now made available free of charge.

A Change of Attitude

Kingston, Ontario, a cold and very old city in Eastern Canada, was called "Stony Kingston" by the missionaries. There had been but one convert to the Church in six years there, even though missionaries had been continuously assigned in that city during the entire time. No one baptized in Kingston. Time in Kingston was marked on the calendar like days in prison. A missionary transfer to another place—any place—would be uppermost in thoughts, even in dreams.

While praying about and pondering this sad dilemma, for my responsibility then as a mission president required that I pray and ponder about such things, my wife called to my attention an excerpt from the book *A Child's Story of the Prophet Brigham Young* by Deta Petersen Neeley (Salt Lake City: Deseret News Press, 1959). She read aloud that Brigham Young entered Kingston, Ontario, on a cold and snow-filled day. He labored there thirty days and baptized forty-five souls. Here was the answer. If the missionary Brigham Young could accomplish this harvest, so could the missionaries of today.

Without providing an explanation, I withdrew the missionaries from Kingston, so that the cycle of defeat might be broken. Then came the carefully circulated word to the missionaries: "Soon a new city will be opened for missionary work, even the city where Brigham Young proselyted and baptized forty-five persons in thirty days." The missionaries speculated as to the location. Their weekly letters pleaded for the assignment to this Shangri-la. More time passed. Then four carefully selected missionaries—two of them new, two of them experienced—were chosen for this high adventure. The members of the small branch pledged their support. The missionaries pledged their efforts. The Lord honored both.

In the space of three months, Kingston became the most productive city of the Canadian Mission. The gray limestone buildings stood unchanged; the city had not altered its appearance; the population remained constant. The change was one of attitude. Doubt had yielded to faith.

A New Elder's Testimony

One of the first accounts I heard when I became president of the Canadian Mission was of the conversion of Elmer Pollard. In the city of Oshawa, Ontario, Canada, two missionaries were proselyting door to door on a cold, snowy afternoon. They had not experienced any measure of success. One had been in the mission field for some time; one was a newly arrived missionary.

The two missionaries called at the home of Elmer Pollard. Feeling sorry for the young men who, during a blinding blizzard, were going house to house, Mr. Pollard invited the missionaries into his home. They presented to him their message. He did not catch the Spirit. In due time he asked that they leave and not return. His last words to the elders as they departed his front porch were spoken in derision: "You can't tell me you actually believe Joseph Smith was a prophet of God!"

He shut the door, and the elders walked down the path. The newly arrived missionary spoke to his companion, "Elder, we didn't respond to Mr. Pollard. He said we didn't believe Joseph Smith was a true prophet. Let's return and bear our testimonies to him."

At first the more experienced missionary was adamant about not returning, but finally he agreed to accompany his "green" companion. Fear struck their hearts as they approached the door from which they had been turned away. Came the knock, the confrontation with Mr. Pollard, an agonizing moment—and then, with power, a testimony born by the Spirit. "Mr. Pollard," began the new missionary, "you said we didn't really believe Joseph Smith was a prophet of God. Mr. Pollard, I testify that Joseph Smith was a prophet; he did translate the Book of Mormon; he saw God the Father and Jesus the Son. I know it."

Mr. Pollard, now Brother Pollard, stood in a priesthood meeting some time later and declared, "That night I could not sleep. Resounding in my ears were the words, 'Joseph Smith was a prophet of God. I know it. I know it.' The next day I telephoned the missionaries. Their message, coupled with their testimonies, changed my life and the lives of my family."

A Message on the Radio

&.

In 1959, when I served as mission president in Canada, the Agnew family was investigating the Church. The missionaries had called and presented their message and the teachings of the gospel. The family studied. They loved what they learned. They were approaching the decision to be baptized.

One Sunday morning, by appointment, the family were preparing to attend Sunday School at the Mormon church. Mother and children readied themselves, but they were disappointed when Dad concluded not to attend. The parents even argued somewhat about the decision. Such was rare, for their home was very harmonious. Then Mother and the children went to Sunday School, and Dad stayed at home.

At first Dad attempted to forget the misunderstanding by reading the newspaper, but to no avail. Then he went to his daughter Isabel's room and turned on the radio on her nightstand, hoping to hear the news. He didn't hear the news. Rather, he heard the Tabernacle Choir broadcast. Elder Richard L. Evans's message, "Let Not the Sun Go Down on Thy Wrath," was, it seemed, directed personally to him.

Brother Agnew realized the futility of his anger. He was now overpowered by a feeling of gratitude for the message he had just received. When his wife and family returned home, they found him pleasant and happy. His children asked how this change had come about. He told them how he had turned on the radio, hoping to get the news, only to be humbled by the message of the Tabernacle Choir in word and song.

His daughter asked, "Which radio did you use, Dad?"

He answered, "The one on your nightstand."

She replied, "That radio is broken. It hasn't played for weeks."

He then led them to the room to prove that this radio did indeed function. He turned the proper knob, but the radio failed to work. Yet when an honest seeker after truth needed the help of God, that radio had worked. The message that led to conversion had been received.

Promise to a New Missionary

There sat in my office one day in Toronto, Ontario, a newly arrived missionary. He was bright, strong, filled with enthusiasm and a desire to serve, happy and grateful to be a missionary. I spoke with him, as his mission president: "Elder, I imagine that your father and mother wholeheartedly support you in your mission call." He lowered his head and replied, "Well, not quite. You see, President, my father is not a member of the Church. He doesn't believe as we believe, so he cannot fully appreciate the importance of my assignment."

Without hesitating, and prompted by a source not my own, I said to him, "Elder, if you will honestly and diligently serve God in proclaiming His message, your father will join the Church before your mission is concluded." He clasped my hand in a vise-like grip. The tears welled up in his eyes and began to roll forth down his cheeks as he declared, "To see my father accept the truth would be the greatest blessing that could come into my life."

This young man did not sit idly by, hoping and wishing that the promise would be fulfilled, but rather he followed the example of Abraham Lincoln, of whom it has been said, "When he prayed, he prayed as though everything depended upon God, and then he worked as though everything depended upon him." Such was the missionary service of this young man.

At every missionary conference I would seek him out before the meetings commenced and ask, "Elder, how's your father progressing?"

His reply would invariably be "No progress, President,

but I know the Lord will fulfill the promise given to me through you as my mission president."

The days turned to weeks and the weeks to months, and finally, just two weeks before my wife and I left the mission field to return home, I received the following letter from the missionary's father:

> *Dear Brother Monson:*
>
> *I wish to thank you so much for taking such good care of my son who recently completed a mission in Canada. He has been an inspiration to us.*
>
> *My son was promised when he arrived in the mission field that I would become a member of the Church before his return. This promise was, I believe, made to him by you, unknown to me.*
>
> *I am happy to report that I was baptized into the Church one week before he completed his mission and am at present time Athletic Director of the MIA and have a teaching assignment.*
>
> *My son is now attending BYU, and his younger brother was also recently baptized and confirmed a member of the Church.*
>
> *May I again thank you for all the kindness and love bestowed upon my son by his brothers in the mission field during the past two years.*
>
>

Yours very truly,
A grateful father
>

The humble prayer of faith had once again been answered.

Hope for a Discouraged Missionary

As a mission president, I was afforded the privilege of guiding the activities of precious young men and women, missionaries whom the Lord had called. Some had problems, others required motivation; but one came to me in utter despair. He had made his decision to leave the mission field when but at the halfway mark. His bags were packed, his return ticket purchased. He came by to bid me farewell. We talked; we listened; we prayed. There remained hidden the actual reason for his decision to quit.

As we arose from our knees in the quiet of my office, the missionary began to weep almost uncontrollably. Flexing the muscle of his strong right arm, he blurted out, "This is my problem. All through school my muscle power qualified me for honors in football and track, but my mental power was neglected. President Monson, I'm ashamed of my school record. It reveals that 'with effort' I have the capacity to read at but the level of the fourth grade. I can't even read the Book of Mormon. How then can I understand its contents and teach others its truths?"

The silence of the room was broken by my nine-year-old son who, without knocking, opened the door and, with surprise, apologetically said, "Excuse me. I just wanted to put this book back on the shelf."

He handed me the book. Its title: *A Child's Story of the Book of Mormon,* by Deta Petersen Neeley. I turned to the preface and read that the book had been written with a carefully selected vocabulary on a fourth-grade level. A sincere prayer from an honest heart had been dramatically answered.

My missionary accepted the challenge to read the book. Half laughing, half crying, he declared: "It will be good to read something I can understand."

Clouds of despair were dispelled by the sunshine of hope. He completed an honorable mission, is now married for eternity to a choice companion, and has children of his own. His life is a testimony of the nearness of our Father and the availability of His help.

A Chapel for St. Thomas

When I first visited the St. Thomas Branch of the Canadian Mission, which was situated about one hundred and twenty miles from Toronto, my wife and I had been invited to attend the branch sacrament meeting and to speak to the members there. As we drove along a fashionable street, we saw many church buildings and wondered which one was ours. None was. We located the address that had been provided and discovered it to be a decrepit lodge hall. Our branch met in the basement of the lodge hall and was comprised of perhaps twenty-five members, about half of whom were in attendance. The same individuals conducted the meeting, blessed and passed the sacrament, offered the prayers, and sang the songs.

At the conclusion of the services, the branch president, Irving Wilson, asked if he could meet with me. At this meeting, he handed to me a copy of the *Improvement Era*, forerunner of today's *Ensign*. Pointing to a picture of one of our new chapels in Australia, President Wilson declared, "This is the building we need here in St. Thomas."

I smiled and responded, "When we have enough members here to justify and to pay for such a building, I am sure we will have one." At that time, the local members were required to raise 30 percent of the cost of the site and the building, in addition to the payment of tithing and other offerings.

He countered, "Our children are growing to maturity. We need that building, and we need it now!"

I provided encouragement for them to grow in numbers by their personal efforts to fellowship and teach. The

147

outcome is a classic example of faith, coupled with effort and crowned with testimony.

President Wilson requested six additional missionaries to be assigned to St. Thomas. When this was accomplished, he called the missionaries to a meeting in the back room of his small jewelry store, where they all knelt in prayer. He then asked one elder to hand to him the yellow-page telephone directory, which was on a nearby table. President Wilson took the book in hand and observed, "If we are ever to have our dream building in St. Thomas, we will need a Latter-day Saint to design it. Since we do not have a member who is an architect, we will simply have to convert one." With his finger moving down the column of listed architects, he paused at one name and said, "This is the one we will invite to my home to hear the message of the Restoration."

President Wilson followed the same procedure with regard to plumbers, electricians, and craftsmen of every description. Nor did he neglect other professions, feeling a desire for a well-balanced branch. The individuals were invited to his home to meet the missionaries, the truth was taught, testimonies were borne, and conversion resulted. Those newly baptized then repeated the procedure themselves, inviting others to listen, week after week and month after month.

The St. Thomas Branch experienced marvelous growth. Within two and one-half years, a site was obtained, a beautiful building was constructed, and an inspired dream became a living reality. That branch became a thriving ward in a stake of Zion.

When I reflect on the town of St. Thomas, I dwell not on the ward's hundreds of members and many dozens of families; rather, in memory I return to that sparsely attended sacrament meeting in the lodge-hall basement and the Lord's promise, "Where two or three are gathered together in my name, there am I in the midst of them." (Matthew 18:20.)

Motivation to Arise

&

We had a missionary in the Canadian Mission who was particularly devoted and obedient. I said to him one time, "Elder, what is the source of your motivation?"

"Brother Monson," he replied, "I slept in one morning. As I did so, my mind turned to thoughts of my mother and my father, who are operating a little cleaning establishment, practically working around the clock to earn sufficient money to support me on a mission. As I thought of my mother and my father performing that strenuous work in my behalf, all signs of laziness left me, and I determined that I had an opportunity to serve the Lord in my behalf and in behalf of my own mother and my own father."

A Five-year-old Missionary

❧

Our daughter, Ann, turned five shortly after we arrived in Canada, where I served as mission president. She saw the missionaries going about their work and she too wanted to be a missionary. My wife demonstrated understanding by permitting Ann to take to class a few copies of the *Children's Friend*. That wasn't sufficient for Ann. She wanted to take a copy of the Book of Mormon, and she talked to her teacher, Miss Pepper, about the Church.

I thought it rather thrilling that long years after our return from Toronto, we came home from a vacation and found in our mailbox a note from Miss Pepper that read:

> *Dear Ann,*
>
> *Think back many years ago. I was your school teacher in Toronto, Canada. I was impressed by the copies of the* Children's Friend *which you brought to school. I was impressed by your dedication to a book called the Book of Mormon.*
>
> *I made a commitment that one day I would come to Salt Lake City and see why you talked as you did and why you believed in the manner you believed. Today I had the privilege of going through your visitors' center on Temple Square. Thanks to a five-year-old girl who had an understanding of that which she believed, I now have a better understanding of The Church of Jesus Christ of Latter-day Saints.*

Miss Pepper died not too long after that visit. How

happy our daughter Ann was when she attended the Jordan River Temple and performed the temple work for her beloved teacher whom she had friendshipped long ago.

A Descendant of Archibald Gardner

One of the great families to join the Church in Canada was that of Archibald Gardner. From his journal, we learn of the family's experience in London, Ontario, Canada, during the year 1843.

Robert Gardner describes the day of their baptism: "We went about a mile and a half into the woods to find a suitable stream. We cut a hole through ice eighteen inches thick. My brother William baptized me. . . . I was confirmed while sitting on a log beside the stream. . . .

"I cannot describe my feelings at the time and for a long time afterwards. I felt like a little child and was very careful of what I thought or said or did lest I might offend my Father in Heaven. Reading the Scriptures and secret prayer occupied my leisure time. I kept a pocket Testament constantly with me. When something on a page impressed me supporting Mormonism, I turned down a corner. Soon I could hardly find a desired passage. I had nearly all the pages turned down. I had no trouble believing the Book of Mormon. Every time I took the book to read I had a burning testimony in my bosom of its truthfulness."

Archibald Gardner added, "[My] mother . . . [accepted] the Gospel at once and whole heartedly, after hearing it. . . . Not long after contacting the new faith she became desperately ill, so ill that her life was despaired of. She insisted on being baptized. The neighbors said that if we put her in the water they would have us tried for murder as she would surely die. Nevertheless, well bundled up, and tucked into a sleigh, we drove her two miles to the place appointed. Here a hole was cut in the ice and she was baptized in the presence of a crowd of doubters who had come to witness her demise. She was taken home. Her bed was prepared but she said, 'No, I do not need to go to bed. I am quite well.' And she was." (Delilah G. Hughes, *The Life of Archibald Gardner,* Draper, Utah: Review and Preview Publishers, 1970, pp. 25-27.)

On one occasion when I was presiding in the Canadian Mission, we had a missionary, Hal Gardner, who had four years of German. I wondered why his mission assignment had not been to Germany. While making a routine transfer within our mission, without knowing the Archibald Gardner story, I assigned Elder Gardner to the London, Ontario, area as the district president. When the members in the town where Archibald Gardner had lived found that Elder Hal Gardner was a descendant of that early pioneer, they had a Gardner family day, with a full-page news story in the paper describing the event. Elder Gardner said, "The Lord knows how to take care of us if we will but put our faith in him."

Hearing Restored

In my early years as a member of the Council of the Twelve, I attended a series of missionary conferences in Australia, one of which was held in Sydney. Following the conference, I spoke to a fireside gathering.

It was necessary that I leave the fireside at an appointed time in order to catch a flight to Auckland, New Zealand, where I was to speak to all the missionaries in that area. When the stake president, William Delves, announced that it would be necessary for me to leave during the closing song, I noticed a look of consternation on the faces of two missionaries seated by the east aisle of the building at Parramatta. As I walked down the aisle, one missionary grasped my hand and said, "Brother Monson, you can't go."

"I must go," I said.

He said, "But who is to give our investigator a blessing?" He pointed to an investigator who sat between the two elders. The man had a hearing aid in each ear.

"You hold all the necessary authority, Elder, that I hold," I said. "You give him the blessing."

The elder replied, "But this man is deaf. We were hopeful that you would restore to him his hearing. In fact, we have told him this could be a definite possibility."

I told the elder, "Since you hold the same power that I hold, if you feel impressed to give him his hearing, you do so, and the Lord will honor your blessing." I then departed the building, was whisked away to the airport, and flew to Auckland, New Zealand.

The next time I attended a quarterly conference of the

Sydney Stake, a young man came up to me following the session and said, "Brother Monson, do you remember me?"

"Your face looks familiar," I responded. "Perhaps I visited with you when I toured this mission six months ago."

"Yes," he said, "you did; but more specifically, I was the missionary who sat on the east aisle, and here is the man who sat next to me. You will recall that at that time he had a hearing aid in each ear, and I mentioned to you his need for a blessing and his desire for a restoration of his hearing. You remember, Brother Monson, you said I held all the priesthood authority that you held, and that if I felt properly inspired, I could bless him and give him his hearing. Bless him I did, and the inspiration came to restore his hearing."

By this time the gentleman said to me, "Elder Monson, I am now a member of The Church of Jesus Christ of Latter-day Saints. When you saw me last, I was deaf, but thanks to the power of the priesthood, the goodness of our Heavenly Father, and the faith of this young man, now I hear."

A Testimony to Prisoners of War

§❧

During World War II, German prisoners of war were incarcerated at Fort Douglas in Salt Lake City. It was against military regulations for visitors to be permitted to speak to the prisoners, nor were they allowed to fraternize with the community.

Kaspar J. Fetzer, native-born German, knew there were German prisoners of war at Fort Douglas; hence, he paid a visit to them. He persuaded the guard to let him talk to the men.

As he visited with the men, he asked if any of them happened to be members of the Church. No one replied affirmatively. Kaspar then took from his pockets copies of the pamphlet "Joseph Smith Tells His Own Story," as published in the German language, and began to give them the first discussion. This occurred in 1944.

In 1969, Percy K. Fetzer and I were reorganizing the presidency of the Hamburg Stake. We interviewed one of the bishops and in the course of that interview learned from him that he had installed a furnace recently in the home of a man who, in the tradition of the German people, offered him a glass of wine after he had completed his mechanical work. The bishop replied that he didn't drink wine. He was then offered beer. He declined the beer and then mentioned that he was a member of the Mormon Church.

The owner of the home said, "I know something about the Mormon Church," and he related that he had been a prisoner of war in the group in Salt Lake City when a wonderful man by the name of Kaspar Fetzer taught to them the Joseph Smith story.

The bishop explained that this discussion opened the way for a visit by the missionaries, and the family entered the waters of baptism.

I said to this fine bishop, "Would you like to meet the son of the man who visited the prisoner of war camp in Salt Lake City?"

"Of course!" he replied.

I then had the opportunity to introduce Percy Fetzer, Kaspar Fetzer's son, to this bishop. What a joy for them to meet and to realize that a choice family had joined the Church as a result of Percy's father's testimony.

We cannot estimate accurately our influence upon others.

A Conversation Remembered

In his seventy-seventh year, Kaspar J. Fetzer was called to leave his wife and business and return to Germany as a missionary, there to help commence the building program.

At his farewell testimonial, his broken English became a handicap. Finally, in exasperation, he struck the pulpit and said, "If there is a German in all Germany who does not want to become a Mormon, he had better stay out of the way of Kaspar J. Fetzer!"

During his mission, he occupied a "No Smoking" compartment on a train as it went from one city to another within Germany. He became well acquainted with a man who sat by his side. The man feigned no interest in the Church, yet enjoyed visiting with Brother Fetzer. This was in 1954.

In 1968, Percy K. Fetzer's son, Robert, a grandson of Kaspar, was a missionary in Brazil. As he and his companion called at one home, the doorkeeper said the master of the home would not be interested. However, the master heard the young men introduce themselves as Mormon missionaries. He then came to the door and invited them in. It turned out to be the same man with whom Kaspar Fetzer had visited on the train in Germany long years before.

Question on a Bus Tour

Years ago I had the opportunity of addressing a business convention in Dallas, Texas, sometimes called "the city of churches." After the convention, I took a sightseeing bus ride about the city's suburbs. Our driver would comment, "On the left you see the Methodist church," or "There on the right is the Catholic cathedral."

As we passed a beautiful red brick building situated upon a hill, the driver exclaimed, "That building is where the Mormons meet." A lady from the rear of the bus asked, "Driver, can you tell us something more about the Mormons?" The driver steered the bus to the side of the road, turned about in his seat, and replied, "Lady, all I know about the Mormons is that they meet in that red brick building. Is there anyone on this bus who knows anything about the Mormons?"

I gazed at the expression on each person's face for some sign of recognition, some desire to comment. I found nothing—not a sign. Then I realized the truth of the statement, "When the time for decision arrives, the time for preparation is past." For the next fifteen minutes I had the privilege of sharing with others my testimony concerning The Church of Jesus Christ of Latter-day Saints.

After I had so borne my testimony, I felt a sweet feeling of peace in my heart, and I was so grateful that I had this opportunity. I thought of the Apostle Peter's counsel, "Be ready always to give an answer to every man that asketh you a reason of the hope that is in you." (1 Peter 3:15.)

Handicapped, Yet Blessed

As a member of the Church's Missionary Executive Committee many years ago, I had the responsibility occasionally to interview marginal candidates for missions. One such person sat in my office one day. His face was horribly scarred, his eyebrows and eyelashes gone. He had been involved in a terrible accident while driving a Volkswagen that overturned. The car caught fire, and this young man was burned nigh unto death.

As I interviewed him, I candidly advised that if he were to respond to a mission call, it would be a most difficult thing for him; for as he was rejected from door to door, due primarily to disinterest in the message, he might think that the rejection came about as the result of his disfigurement. The young man calmly said that he had considered this factor and had adjusted his thinking so that the situation would not be a liability.

I felt within him such a great desire to serve that I made the decision to permit the recommendation to be handled in the usual manner. He was assigned to the Northern California Mission.

After two years I received from his mission president the following letter:

"The bearer of this letter has served in our mission for two years. He has been one of the finest missionaries in our mission over the whole time that he has been here. He has been effective as a leader, as a proselyting missionary, as the liaison between the mission office and the several stakes in which he has served and in all respects his performance has been without flaw.

"He has handled his personal problem, his severe scarring, in a way that has discouraged or affronted no one. It has been on a basis that 'this is my problem; don't you worry about it.'

"We love him dearly. We are grateful for his service; and if you have any more just like him, send them along."

Early in 1971 this same young man came to my office and requested that I perform his marriage ceremony in the temple of the Lord. He had found the girl of his dreams, and together they planned eternal marriage. I performed their marriage that June in the Salt Lake Temple. He is now a successful businessman, and he and his lovely wife are the parents of several children.

A Key to Precious Archives

ॐ

Sister Monson and I had the opportunity of visiting the land of Sweden while her cousin, Reid Johnson, was the mission president, and we heard an account that brought joy to our hearts. As President Johnson and our group were journeying throughout the mission, we went to a large Lutheran church in the town of Granjarde, Sweden. As we walked into the building, President Johnson said, "I think you would be interested in an experience my companion, Richard Timpson, and I had in this city at the termination of our missions back in 1948."

He said, "We came to this town because we knew that our family history was steeped here and had been lived here. As we entered this large church, we were met by a most protective keeper of the archives. Upon hearing that we had completed our missions and had a few precious days in which we would like to seek out the records that he maintained in his church building, he said that no one had ever been given the opportunity to peruse those valuable records, far less a Mormon. He declared they were under lock and key, and he held up to view the large key to the vault in which the records were stored. He said, 'My job and my future, and the sustenance of my family, depend upon how well I safeguard this key. No, I am afraid it would be impossible for you to peruse these records. But if you would like to see the church, I'll be happy to show you through. I'll be glad to show you the architecture and the cemetery that surrounds the church, but not the records, for they are sacred.'"

President Johnson indicated they were stunned, and their hopes had vanished into thin air, but he said to the keeper of the archives, "We will accept your kind offer." All this time President Johnson and his companion were praying fervently and earnestly that somehow something would change the man's mind, that he would let them view the records.

After a lengthy journey through the cemetery and looking at the church building, the keeper of the archives said to them, "I'm going to do something I have never done before. It may cost me my job, but I'm going to let you borrow this key for fifteen minutes."

President Johnson thought, "Fifteen minutes! All we can do in fifteen minutes is open the lock!" But they took the key, opened the lock, and had made available to their view records that were priceless for their genealogical value. In fifteen minutes the keeper arrived. He looked at them and found they were still in a state of Christmas wonder over the find they had discovered.

They asked, "Can't we stay longer?"

He said, "How much longer?" And he looked at his watch.

They replied, "About four days."

He said, "I don't know why, but I feel I can trust you. Here is the key. You keep it, and when you are through, you return it to me. I'll be here every morning at eight o'clock and every evening at five o'clock."

For four consecutive days those two missionaries literally studied and recorded for our current use information that could have been obtained in no other way. President Johnson was filled with emotion as he explained this experience to us. He said, "The Lord does move in a mysterious way, his wonders to perform." As he made this statement of testimony to me, I realized that this was also a blessing that had come to me and my wife, for the information gathered applied to some of our family lines.

"Keep Writing!"

Spiritual strength frequently comes through selfless service. Some years ago I visited the California Mission, where I interviewed a young missionary from Georgia. I recall saying to him, "Do you send a letter home to your parents every week?"

He replied, "Yes, Brother Monson, every week for the last five months."

Then I asked, "Do you enjoy receiving letters from home?"

He didn't answer. I then inquired, "When was the last time you had a letter from home?"

With a quavering voice, he responded, "I've never had a letter from home. Father's just a deacon, and Mother's not a member of the Church. They pleaded with me not to come. They said that if I left on a mission, they would not be writing to me. My aunt is supporting me on my mission. What shall I do?"

I offered a silent prayer to my Heavenly Father: What shall I tell this young servant of Thine, who has sacrificed everything to serve Thee? And the inspiration came. I said, "Elder, you send a letter home to your mother and father every week of your mission. Tell them what you are doing. Tell them how much you love them, and then bear your testimony to them."

He asked, "Will they then write to me?"

I responded, "Then they will write to you."

We parted, and I went on my way. Months later I was attending a stake conference in Southern California when a young man came up to me and said, "Brother Monson, do you remember me? I'm the missionary who had not received a letter from my mother or my father during my first nine months in the mission field. I'm the one to whom you said, 'Send a letter home every week, Elder, and your parents will write to you.'" Then he asked, "Do you remember that promise, Elder Monson?"

I remembered. I inquired, "Have you heard from your parents?"

He reached into his pocket and took out a sheaf of letters with an elastic band around them, took a letter from the top of the stack, and said, "Have I heard from my parents! Listen to this letter from my mother: 'Son, we so much enjoy your letters. We're proud of you, our missionary. Guess what? Dad has been ordained a priest. He's preparing to baptize me. I'm meeting with the missionaries, and one year from now we want to come to California as you complete your mission, for we, with you, would like to become a forever family by entering the temple of the Lord.'" Then the young man put his hand in mine and asked, "Brother Monson, does Heavenly Father always answer prayers and fulfill apostles' promises?"

I replied, "When one has faith as you have demonstrated, our Heavenly Father hears such prayers and answers in His own way."

A blessing, heaven-sent, had answered the fervent prayer of a missionary's humble heart.

"You Must Be a Mormon"

♠

One summer day in 1972, I took a flight from San Francisco to Los Angeles. I was sitting on the first row, and a beautiful young lady was sitting next to me, reading. As one does, I looked over to see what she was reading. How pleased I was when I noted that she was reading *A Marvelous Work and a Wonder* by LeGrand Richards. I said to her, "You must be a Mormon."

She said, "No, sir. Why do you ask?"

I said, "It's the book you're reading, *A Marvelous Work and a Wonder*. It was written by an apostle in the Mormon Church. In fact, I printed the book."

She said, "Well, then, maybe you can answer some questions I have," and she gave me three or four rather interesting questions. I responded as best I could. I learned that she was an off-duty flight attendant with United Airlines, and her name was Yvonne Ramirez. A friend had given her the book.

She continued to read, and I pretended to be reading what I had. The thought came to me that maybe the Lord had put me in the seat next to this young lady, and that perhaps He wanted me to bear my testimony to her. I turned toward her, as the plane was making its approach to the Los Angeles Airport, and bore my testimony. I told her I would send her a book that I had written, along with a pamphlet about the Church. I asked if she would be willing to receive visitors from our church. She said she would be delighted to do so.

The plane landed, and she went her way. When I returned to Salt Lake City, I sent her a copy of one of my books, along with a copy of the pamphlet "Joseph Smith's Testimony." I also called the mission president and the stake president in San Francisco and arranged to have two missionaries call on her.

In September a telephone call came to my home from the stake president in San Francisco. He said, "Remember last summer when you flew on United Airlines from San Francisco to Los Angeles and sat next to an off-duty flight attendant?" I indicated that I did indeed remember and that I remembered her name, Yvonne Ramirez. He said, "That's the one." He said that she had just been baptized and confirmed a member of the Church. "In fact," he told me, "she would like to talk with you. She is the most recently baptized member of the Church. Her hair is still wet."

Then a shy voice came on the line and said, "Brother Monson?"

I said, "Yes."

"This is Yvonne Ramirez. Thank you for sharing with me your testimony. Tonight I am the happiest person in the world!"

A Michigan Sweatshirt

At the funeral services for my friend O. Preston Robinson on November 13, 1990, a man and his wife approached me and asked if they could relate an experience in their family that brought joy to their hearts.

They mentioned that at the BYU Aspen Grove facility the previous July, I had spoken at a Sunday devotional. I noted in the audience a man wearing a sweatshirt bearing a large letter "M" for Michigan. The sweatshirt was gold and blue, the colors of the University of Michigan's athletic uniforms.

I had related to the group that from boyhood I have had a love for the Michigan Wolverines, as they are called. It all began with my first subscription to *Boys' Life* and an article featuring Tom Harmon, the All-American quarterback from Michigan. I briefly mentioned his subsequent career as a war hero and then mentioned a few other highlights of Michigan teams. I commented that my family had given me similar shirts and caps bearing the Michigan symbol, and that during the New Year's Day football games, if Michigan was playing, I would wear one of those shirts and would be ready at the record player to play on a moment's notice the Michigan fight song, "Hail to the Victors."

The couple I met at the funeral then commented that the man who had been wearing the Michigan shirt at the Aspen Grove meeting was their relative. He had never shown much interest in the Church, and they had not as yet found a way to reach his heart.

Then they told me that as a result of my message and

the comments made concerning the University of Michigan at Ann Arbor, the man made a turnabout and invited the missionaries to his home. His conversion to the gospel resulted.

Courage in a Guatemalan Earthquake

$♪$

In early 1976, while serving in Guatemala as a missionary for The Church of Jesus Christ of Latter-day Saints, Randall Ellsworth survived a devastating earthquake that hurled a beam down on his back, paralyzed his legs, and severely damaged his kidneys. He was the only American injured in the quake, which claimed the lives of 18,000 persons.

After receiving emergency medical treatment, he was flown to a hospital near his home in Rockville, Maryland. While he was confined there, a television newscaster conducted an interview with him that I witnessed through the miracle of television. The reporter asked, "Can you walk?"

The answer: "Not yet, but I will."

"Do you think you will be able to complete your mission?"

Came the reply, "Others think not, but I will."

With microphone in hand, the reporter continued, "I understand you have received a special letter containing a get-well message from the President of the United States."

"Yes," replied Randall, "I am very grateful to President Ford for his thoughtfulness. But I received another letter, not from the president of my country, but from the president of my church—The Church of Jesus Christ of Latter-day Saints—President Spencer W. Kimball. This I cherish. With him praying for me, and the prayers of my family, my friends, and my missionary companions, I will return to Guatemala. The Lord wanted me to preach the gospel there for two years, and that's what I intend to do."

I turned to my wife and commented, "He surely must

not know the extent of his injuries. Our official medical reports would not permit us to expect such a return to Guatemala."

How grateful I am that the day of faith and the age of miracles are not past history but continue with us even now.

The newspapers and the television cameras turned their attention to more immediate news as the days turned to weeks and the weeks to months. But God did not forget him who possessed a humble and a contrite heart, even Elder Randall Ellsworth. Little by little the feeling began to return to his legs. In his own words, Randall described the recovery: "The thing I did was always to keep busy, always pushing myself. In the hospital I asked to do therapy twice a day instead of just once. I wanted to walk again on my own."

When the Missionary Department evaluated the amazing medical progress Randall Ellsworth had made, word was sent to him that his return to Guatemala was authorized. "At first I was so happy I didn't know what to do," he said. "Then I went into my bedroom, and I started to cry. Then I dropped to my knees and thanked my Heavenly Father."

In the summer of 1976 Randall Ellsworth walked, with the aid of two canes, aboard the plane that carried him back to the mission to which he was called and back to the people he loved. His walk was slow and deliberate. Then one day, as he stood before his mission president, John Forres O'Donnal, Randall Ellsworth heard President O'Donnal speak the almost unbelievable words: "You have been the recipient of a miracle. Your faith has been rewarded. If you have the necessary confidence, if you have abiding faith, if you have supreme courage, place those two canes on my desk—and walk."

Slowly, Randall placed one cane and then the other on the mission president's desk, turned toward the door, and toward his future—and walked.

Following his mission, Randall Ellsworth pursued schooling and eventually became a practicing physician as well as a stalwart husband and a loving father.

His mission president, John Forres O'Donnal—the man who helped bring to Guatemala the word of the Lord—visited my office one day and, in his modest manner, recounted his experience with Randall Ellsworth. He then said to me, "Together we have witnessed a miracle. I have kept one of the two canes placed upon my desk that day when I challenged Elder Ellsworth to walk without them. I would like you to have the other." With a friendly smile, he departed the office and returned home to Guatemala.

The cane given to me served as a silent witness of our Heavenly Father's ability to hear our prayers and to bless our lives. It was a symbol of faith, a reminder of courage.

One day some time later, Randall walked into my office for a visit, along with his lovely wife and their children. When he left, I returned the cane to him, with a silent prayer of gratitude in my heart for the blessings of a loving Heavenly Father to a modern-day Paul who had also overcome his "thorn in the flesh." (2 Corinthians 12:7.)

Inspiration from a Funeral

In December of 1970, I spoke at the funeral service of Melvin Woodbury, husband of my mother's cousin, Agnes Poulton Woodbury. Mel's passing was very sudden. Franklin D. Richards, a business associate of Brother Woodbury's, and I were asked to be the speakers.

During the viewing prior to the funeral service, I greeted Agnes's sisters, particularly Blanche and her husband Felix (Pete) Peterson, sixty-nine years of age, who was not a member of the Church.

During the funeral service I felt a particularly sacred influence directing my remarks. It seemed as though the words came from God and that I had full power of expression. The family seemed comforted. I felt humbled and grateful.

Two weeks later, Agnes Woodbury came to my office. She said that her brother-in-law, Pete Peterson, had suddenly come to his wife and his two sons, Kenneth, on the high council, and Norman, stake Sunday School superintendent, and announced that he was ready to become a member of the Church. He attributed his conversion to my message that he had heard and the other influences surrounding the funeral service of Melvin Woodbury.

One son baptized him; another confirmed him. I expressed to Agnes and to the Lord my gratitude and ascribed to Him the honor and glory of any accomplishment.

Saved Slides

ॐ

Brother Edwin Q. Cannon, Jr., was a missionary in 1938 to Germany, where he loved the people and served faithfully. At the conclusion of his mission, he returned home to Salt Lake City.

Forty years passed by. One day Brother Cannon came to my office and said he had been pruning his missionary slides. Among those slides he had kept since his mission were several he could not specifically identify. Every time he had planned to discard them, he had been impressed to keep them, although he was at a loss as to why.

The photographs had been taken by Brother Cannon during his mission when he served in Stettin, Germany, and were of a family—a mother, a father, a small girl, a small boy. He knew their surname was Berndt, but he could remember nothing more about them. He indicated that he understood there was a Berndt who was a regional representative in Germany, and he thought, although the possibility was remote, that this Berndt might have some connection with the Berndts who had lived in Stettin and who were depicted in the photographs. Before disposing of the slides, he thought he would check with me.

I told Brother Cannon I was leaving shortly for Berlin, where I anticipated that I would see Dieter Berndt, the regional representative, and that I would show the slides to him to see if there were any relationship and if he wanted them. There was a possibility I would also see Brother Berndt's sister, who was married to Dietmar Matern, a stake president in Hamburg.

The Lord didn't even let me get to Berlin before His

purposes were accomplished. I was in Zurich, Switzerland, boarding the flight to Berlin, when who should also board the plane but Dieter Berndt. He sat next to me, and I told him I had some old slides of people named Berndt from Stettin. I handed them to him and asked if he could identify the people in them.

As he looked at them carefully, he began to weep. He said, "Our family lived in Stettin during the war. My father was killed when an Allied bomb struck the plant where he worked. Not long afterward, the Russians invaded Poland and the area of Stettin. My mother took my sister and me and fled from the advancing enemy. Everything had to be left behind, including any photographs we had. I am the little boy pictured in these slides, and my sister is the little girl. The man and woman are our dear parents. Until today, I have had no photographs of our childhood in Stettin or of my father."

Wiping away my own tears, I told Brother Berndt the slides were his. He placed them carefully and lovingly in his briefcase.

At the next general conference, when Dieter Berndt visited Salt Lake City, he paid a visit to Brother and Sister Edwin Cannon, Jr., so that he might express in person his gratitude for the inspiration that had come to Brother Cannon to retain those precious slides and the inspiration Brother Cannon had followed in keeping them for forty years.

An Elder's Courage

ℰ

Elder Thomas Michael Wilson of Lafayette, Alabama, completed his earthly mission on January 13, 1990. When he was a teenager and he and his family were not yet members of the Church, he was stricken with cancer, followed by painful radiation therapy, and then blessed remission. This illness caused his family to realize that not only is life precious but that it can also be short.

The family began to look to religion to help them through this time of tribulation. Subsequently they were introduced to the Church and all were baptized except the father. After accepting the gospel, Thomas yearned for the opportunity to be a missionary. A mission call came for him to serve in the Utah Salt Lake City Mission. What a privilege to represent his family and the Lord as a missionary!

Elder Wilson's missionary companions described his faith as like that of a child—unquestioning, undeviating, unyielding. He was an example to all. However, after eleven months, illness returned. Bone cancer now required the amputation of his arm and shoulder. Yet he persisted in his missionary labors.

Elder Wilson's courage and consuming desire to remain on his mission so touched his nonmember father that he investigated the teachings of the Church and also became a member.

An anonymous caller brought to my attention Elder Wilson's situation. She said she didn't want to leave her name and indicated she'd never before called a General Authority. However, she said, "You don't often meet someone of the caliber of Elder Wilson."

I learned that an investigator whom Elder Wilson had taught had been baptized at the baptistry on Temple Square and then wanted to be confirmed by Elder Wilson, whom she respected so much. She, with a few others, journeyed to Elder Wilson's bedside in the hospital. There, with his remaining hand resting upon her head, Elder Wilson confirmed her a member of The Church of Jesus Christ of Latter-day Saints.

Elder Wilson continued month after month his precious but painful service as a missionary. Blessings were given him, prayers were offered in his behalf. The spirit of his fellow missionaries soared. Their hearts were full. They lived closer to God.

Then Elder Wilson's physical condition deteriorated. The end drew near and he was scheduled to return home. He asked to serve but one additional month. What a month this was! Like a child trusting implicitly its parents, Elder Wilson put his trust in God. He whom Thomas Michael Wilson silently trusted opened the windows of heaven and abundantly blessed him.

Elder Wilson's parents and his brother came to Salt Lake City to help their son and brother home to Alabama. However, there was yet a prayed-for, a yearned-for, blessing to be bestowed. The family invited me to come with them to the Jordan River Temple, where those sacred ordinances which bind families for eternity, as well as for time, were performed.

I said good-bye to the Wilson family. I can see Elder Wilson yet as he thanked me for being with him and his loved ones. He said, "It doesn't matter what happens to us in this life as long as we have the gospel of Jesus Christ and live it." What courage! What confidence! What love! The

Wilson family made the long trek home to Lafayette, where Elder Thomas Michael Wilson slipped from here to eternity.

President Kevin K. Meadows, Elder Wilson's branch president, presided at the funeral services. In a letter to me, he wrote: "On the day of the funeral, I took the family aside and expressed to them, President Monson, the sentiments you sent to me in your letter. I reminded them of what Elder Wilson had told you that day in the temple, that it did not matter whether he taught the gospel on this or the other side of the veil, so long as he could teach the gospel. I gave to them the inspiration you provided from the writings of President Joseph F. Smith—that Elder Wilson had completed his earthly mission and that all 'faithful elders of this dispensation, when they depart from mortal life, continue their labors in the preaching of the gospel of repentance and redemption, through the sacrifice of the Only Begotten Son of God, among those who are in darkness and under the bondage of sin in the great world of the spirits of the dead.' [D&C 138:57.] The Spirit bore record that this was the case. Elder Thomas Michael Wilson was buried with his missionary name tag in place."

When Elder Wilson's mother and his father visit that rural cemetery and place flowers of remembrance on the grave of their son, I feel certain they will remember the day he was born, the pride they felt, and the genuine joy that was theirs. This tiny child they will remember became the mighty man who later brought to them the opportunity to achieve celestial glory. Perhaps on these pilgrimages, when emotions are close to the surface and tears cannot be restrained, they will again thank God for their missionary son who never lost the faith of a child, and then ponder deep within their hearts the Master's words: "And a little child shall lead them." (Isaiah 11:6.)

A Grateful Convert

In 1990 I attended a priesthood leadership session in Basel, Switzerland, for the Zurich-Munich Region. Regional Representative Johann Wondra, later a temple president, arose and spoke to the audience. He invited Brother Kuno Müller, who was seated near the front of the building, to stand.

Brother Wondra told the congregation, "Here is the missionary who brought the gospel and all that it means to my wife and me. Without him, where would I be?" He then turned to Brother Müller and said, "Brother Müller, I love you. My family and I think of you every day. There has never been a day since we met you that we have not dropped to our knees and thanked Heavenly Father for your testimony and for your teachings of the gospel of Christ."

Both Brother Wondra and Brother Müller were weeping. In fact, we all had moist eyes because we had seen an expression of gratitude on the part of one who had received eternal truths, as expressed to the messenger who brought those truths.

The next morning at the conclusion of the general session, Brother Müller, still a missionary, introduced to us a new family of investigators with whom he was working as a stake missionary, and he was still crying when he said, "And they have accepted baptism and will become members of the true church."

Dedication of Portugal

In April of 1975, I received the assignment to dedicate the land of Portugal for the preaching of the gospel. Portugal had not had missionaries through its long years of history, but after much effort and negotiation, permission was granted for missionaries to be assigned to this land.

While on assignment in Sweden, I received a telephone call from President W. Grant Bangerter, president of the Portugal Lisbon Mission, who urged that I come to Portugal immediately to offer a prayer of dedication, rather than waiting until the appointed assignment date. I inquired as to his anxiety. He revealed that a general election was to take place in two days' time that could have a very marked effect on the establishment of the Church in that land. There was a ground swell of opposition against a conservative government.

Sister Monson and I flew to Lisbon and were met by President Bangerter, about ten or twelve members of the Church, and a handful of missionaries. The commodious hotel where we stayed was largely vacant, as preelection fear of violence gripped the hearts of the populace.

The next morning, atop a hillside, our small party gathered. Just as I was about to offer the prayer of dedication, President Bangerter said, "Ask our Heavenly Father to take charge of the election, that the Church may remain in Portugal and fulfill its destiny among this people." In the prayer of dedication, I importuned our Heavenly Father to watch over the land and to bless the people with an outcome in the election that would be beneficial to the presentation of the gospel of Jesus Christ.

Two days later in Europe, I read the Paris edition of the *Herald Tribune,* which carried a headline, "Moderates Sweep Portugal Election!"

From that point of dedication, the membership grew dramatically, with a very bright future in store.

Another Elder Monson

The seeds of testimony frequently do not take root and flower at once. Bread cast upon the water returns, at times, only after many days.

I answered the ring of my telephone one evening to hear a voice ask, "Are you related to an Elder Monson who years ago served in the New England Mission?" I answered that such was not the case.

The caller introduced himself as a Brother Leonardo Gambardella and mentioned that an Elder Monson and an Elder Bonner called at his home long ago and bore their personal testimonies to him. He had listened but had done nothing further to apply their teachings. Subsequently he moved to California, where, after thirteen years, he again found the truth and was converted and baptized.

Brother Gambardella then asked if there were a way he could reach these elders who first had visited with him, so that he might express to them his profound gratitude for their testimonies, which had remained with him.

I checked the records. I located the elders, now married with families of their own. Can you imagine their surprise when I telephoned them and told them the good news— even the culmination of their early efforts? They remembered Brother Gambardella and, at my suggestion, telephoned him to extend their congratulations and welcome him into the Church.

TESTIMONY TEACHES TRUTH

*Be ready always to give an answer
to every man that asketh you
a reason of the hope that is in you.*

1 PETER 3:15

First Talk

When, as a young boy, I was asked to give my first talk, I was given the liberty of choosing any subject I wanted. I have always liked birds, so I thought of the Seagull Monument.

In preparation, I went to Temple Square and looked at the Seagull Monument. First of all, I was attracted to all the coins in the water and tried to figure out how to get the coins out without being seen. Then I looked upward at the seagull perched atop that monument and tried to imagine what it would be like to be a pioneer watching the first year's harvest of grain being devoured by crickets and then seeing those seagulls, with their lofty wings, descending upon the fields and eating the crickets. I loved the story, and I sat down with a lead pencil and wrote out a two-and-one-half-minute talk.

I've never forgotten the seagulls, I've never forgotten the crickets, I've never forgotten my knees knocking together during that two-and-one-half-minute talk. I've never forgotten the experience of letting some of my innermost feelings be expressed verbally at the pulpit. How important it is for youth to be given an opportunity to think, to reason, to speak, and to serve.

A Lesson about Sacrament and Welfare

&

My introduction to the welfare program came when I was a deacon at twelve years of age. The bishop asked that I take the sacrament to a bedfast brother who longed for this blessing. The morning was sunny, and I didn't mind missing my Sunday School class to walk the three-quarters of a mile distance from the chapel, down the street, across the railroad tracks to the modest residence. I knocked at the kitchen door and heard a feeble voice say, "Come in."

I entered the kitchen, then moved to the bedside of Brother Edward Wright. When I uncovered the sacrament, he asked if I would place a piece of bread in his shaking hand and press the cup of water to his trembling lips. His gratitude overwhelmed me. The Spirit of the Lord came over me. I stood on sacred ground.

Brother Wright then asked that I sit and stay awhile. He said, "Tommy, this church is divine. The love the members have one for another is an inspiration. Take, for example, our Relief Society president, Sister Balmforth. Do you know what she did one week many years ago? She took her little red wagon, went to members' homes, and gathered a jar of peaches here, a can of vegetables there, and brought to my cupboard shelves the food that sustained me." I remember that Brother Wright cried as he told of the experience and described watching the Relief Society president walk away from his home pulling behind her, over the bumpy railroad tracks, the red wagon of mercy.

I left that humble home and skipped back to the chapel—the same chapel where, ten years later, I would be sustained as the bishop, presiding over a membership that, more than any other in the Church, needed the welfare program.

"Have Courage, My Boy"

The general session of the Temple View Stake conference was being held in the Assembly Hall. Our stake presidency was to be reorganized. Members of the Aaronic Priesthood, including the bishoprics, were providing the music for the conference, and as a bishop, I too was singing in the chorus.

As we concluded singing our first selection, President Joseph Fielding Smith, our conference visitor, stepped to the pulpit and read for sustaining approval the names of the new stake presidency, including my name. I am confident the other members of the stake presidency had been made aware of their callings, but I had not. After reading my name, President Smith announced: "If Brother Monson is willing to respond to this call, we shall be pleased to hear from him now."

As I stood at the pulpit and gazed out on that sea of faces, I remembered the song we had just sung. Its title was "Have Courage, My Boy, to Say No." That day I selected as my acceptance theme "Have Courage, My Boy, to Say Yes." I have been saying yes ever since.

"Arthur Lives!"

During the time World War II raged, Mrs. Terese Patton was proud of the blue star that graced her living room window, representing to every passerby that her son Arthur, my boyhood friend, wore the uniform of his country. When I would pass the house, she often opened the door and invited me in to hear the latest letter from Arthur. She would read until her eyes filled with tears, and I would then be asked to read aloud.

Arthur had blond, curly hair and a smile as big as all outdoors. He stood taller than any boy in the class. I suppose this is how he was able to fool the recruiting officers and enlist in the Navy at age fifteen.

To Arthur and most of the boys, the war was a great adventure. I remember how striking he appeared in his Navy uniform. How we wished we were older, or at least taller, so we too could enlist.

Arthur meant everything to his widowed mother. I can still picture Mrs. Patton's coarse hands as she would carefully replace the letter in its envelope. These were honest hands that bore the worker's seal. Mrs. Patton was a cleaning woman in a downtown office building. Each day except Sundays, she could be seen walking up the sidewalk, pail and brush in hand, her gray hair combed in a tight bob, her shoulders weary from work and stooped with age.

Then one day she received the dreaded news that Arthur had died at sea. The blue star was taken from its hallowed spot in the front window. It was replaced by one of gold. A light went out in the life of Mrs. Patton. She groped in darkness and deep despair.

With a prayer in my heart, I approached the familiar walkway to the Patton home, wondering what words of comfort could come from the lips of a mere boy. The door opened, and Mrs. Patton embraced me as she would her own son. Home became a chapel as a grief-stricken mother and a less-than-adequate boy knelt in prayer.

As we arose from our knees, Mrs. Patton gazed into my eyes and spoke: "Tom, I know that you are a religious young man. Tell me, will Arthur live again?"

I do not recall the exact words of comfort I spoke to her that day. However, years later, in 1969, as I spoke in general conference, I addressed my remarks to Mrs. Patton and said, "Mrs. Patton, wherever you are, from the backdrop of my personal experience, I should like to once more answer your question, 'Will Arthur live again?'"

I mentioned the words of the Psalmist: "If I take the wings of the morning, and dwell in the uttermost parts of the sea; even there shall thy hand lead me, and thy right hand shall hold me." (Psalm 139:9-10.)

I quoted the words of the Savior, as well as the testimony of John the revelator when he said, "I saw the dead, small and great, stand before God; . . . and the sea gave up the dead which were in it." (Revelation 20:12-13.)

At the conclusion of my address, I added the testimony of a witness, saying, "Mrs. Patton, God our Father is mindful of you. Through sincere prayer you can communicate with Him. He too had a Son who died, even Jesus Christ the Lord. He is our advocate with the Father, the Prince of Peace, our Savior and Divine Redeemer. One day we shall see Him face to face. In His blessed name I declare to you the solemn and sacred truth: Oh, Mrs. Patton, Arthur lives!"

Following the broadcast of that message, I received a

touching letter from Mrs. Terese Patton, Arthur's mother, who was living in Pomona, California. Among other things, she wrote, "I don't know how to thank you for your wonderful and comforting words. God bless you always."

Appreciating the Melchizedek Priesthood

♔

When I was approaching my eighteenth birthday and preparing to enter military service near the close of World War II, I was recommended to receive the Melchizedek Priesthood. Mine was the task of telephoning my stake president, Paul C. Child, for an appointment and interview. He was one who loved and understood the holy scriptures. It was his intent that all others should similarly love and understand them. Knowing from others of his rather detailed and searching interviews, my telephone conversation with him went something like this:

"Hello, President Child. This is Tom Monson. I have been asked by the bishop to seek an interview with you."

"Fine, Brother Monson. When can you visit me?"

Knowing that his sacrament meeting time was six o'clock, and desiring minimum exposure of my scriptural knowledge to his review, I suggested, "How would Sunday at five o'clock be?"

His response: "Oh, Brother Monson, that would not provide us sufficient time to peruse the scriptures. Could you please come at two o'clock, and bring with you your personally marked and referenced set of scriptures."

Sunday finally arrived, and I visited President Child's home on Indiana Avenue. I was greeted warmly, and then the interview began. He said, "Brother Monson, you hold the Aaronic Priesthood. Have you ever had angels minister to you?"

My reply was: "No, President Child."

"Do you know," said he, "that you are entitled to such?"

Again came my response: "No."

Then he instructed, "Brother Monson, repeat from memory the thirteenth section of the Doctrine and Covenants."

I began, "Upon you my fellow servants, in the name of the Messiah I confer the Priesthood of Aaron, which holds the keys of the ministering of angels. . . ." (D&C 13:1.)

"Stop," President Child directed. Then in a calm, kindly tone he counseled: "Brother Monson, never forget that as a holder of the Aaronic Priesthood, you are entitled to the ministering of angels." It was almost as if an angel were in the room that day. I have never forgotten the interview. I yet feel the spirit of that solemn occasion. I revere the priesthood of Almighty God. I have witnessed its power. I have seen its strength. I have marveled at the miracles it has wrought.

Counsel from Harold B. Lee

Toward the end of World War II, I enlisted in the United States Naval Reserve. My training took place at the Naval Training Center, San Diego, California, where I later became attached to that facility on a permanent basis. As the months went by, I worked diligently to achieve the rank of Seaman First Class. I had excellent opportunities at the Naval Training Center serving as the personal secretary and administrative aide to the classification officer, Lt. Commander Joseph M. Santos.

One thing I did learn in the Navy was that the commissioned officers represented a privileged class, followed by the petty officers, with those below the rank of petty officer being grouped together with fewer privileges. Upon my discharge from the Navy, I reenrolled at the University of Utah and later entered the United States Naval Reserve unit at Fort Douglas, Utah, so that I might qualify to receive a commission in the United States Naval Reserve. I felt this was added insurance so that if there should be another conflict, I would at least have the opportunity to be a commissioned officer.

I labored to qualify in every respect for consideration as a commissioned officer. Upon graduating from the University of Utah, I submitted a list of my credits, a personal reference from my employment supervisor from several summers earlier at the United States Naval Supply Depot, Clearfield, Utah, and any other personal reference I could obtain in order to make my application as impressive as possible. My first application brought forth a request for additional information. This I obtained and then awaited the outcome.

In the meantime, my wife, Frances, and I were living at 508 South Second West and were members of the Sixth-Seventh Ward of the Temple View Stake. In March of 1950, there arrived in the mail from Washington, D.C., my commission as an ensign in the United States Naval Reserve. It was a beautiful certificate with my name in script lettering, and then those words I had long desired to see: a commissioned officer. At last my ambition had been achieved. Contained in the cover letter was a statement to the effect that I had thirty days to accept the commission. I smiled at this sentence, realizing how strenuously I had labored to qualify.

Within days, Bishop John R. Burt came to our home and extended to me a call to serve as second counselor in the bishopric of the Sixth-Seventh Ward. He mentioned that our bishopric meeting would convene each Monday night at seven o'clock. Immediately I recognized that this was the exact time that my Naval Reserve drill meeting was held, but I determined to say nothing.

After praying and worrying about the conflict between my reserve obligations and my new position as a member of the bishopric, I determined to visit with my former stake president and revered Church leader, Elder Harold B. Lee. As I sat in Brother Lee's office, I explained to him that I was a member of the Naval Reserve and held the rating of yeoman third class and that I had just received a commission in the Naval Reserve as an ensign. He, of course, knew of my call to the bishopric inasmuch as he had set me apart to this position.

I explained to Brother Lee that war clouds were on the horizon in the Far East, and that if our headquarters unit of the Naval Reserve were to be activated, I no doubt would be called to active duty. Elder Lee pondered for a few minutes and then leaned toward me and said, "Brother Monson, place that commission in an envelope and mail it back to Washington, D.C., with a letter indicating that you are not in a position to accept it. Then write a letter to the commanding officer of the Twelfth Naval District in San Francisco, to which your reserve unit is attached, and indicate that you would like to be discharged from the reserve."

I responded, "Elder Lee, you don't understand. There will be no problem at Washington, D.C., in withdrawing the commission that has been extended to me, but I have no reason to think that the Twelfth Naval District will in any way honor my request for discharge from the Reserve."

Elder Lee countered, "Brother Monson, have more faith. The military is not for you."

I returned to my office and the activities of that day feeling that Brother Lee surely did not understand the complexities involved in my situation. However, I so respected his judgment that I complied with his counsel. With tears in my eyes, I posted to Washington, D.C., the beautiful commission and a letter indicating that I could not accept the commission of an ensign in the United States Naval Reserve. I then sent a letter to the commander of the Twelfth Naval District requesting discharge from my reserve unit.

Within a few weeks, my discharge through San Francisco arrived in the mail. My discharge was among the last processed before the Korean War broke out in all its fury and my Naval Reserve unit at Fort Douglas was activated and sent to the Far East.

Within seven weeks of my call as second counselor in the bishopric, our bishop was called to serve in the stake presidency and I was called to serve as the bishop of the ward. Again I went in to see Elder Lee and told him the outcome of the counsel he had provided. Brother Lee smiled and said, "There is safety, Tom, in following the servants of the Lord. Had you not followed the counsel I provided, difficult as it may have appeared to you at the time, you would not have been called by the Lord to be the bishop of your ward."

I have often contemplated what the course of my life might have been had I not received and followed the advice of Elder Lee. I pondered the thought that the wisdom of God ofttimes appears as foolishness to men. But the greatest single lesson we can learn in mortality is that when God speaks and a man obeys, that man will always be right.

The Worth of a Soul

§

Early in my service as a member of the Council of the Twelve, I was attending the conference of the Monument Park West Stake in Salt Lake City. My companion for the conference was a member of the General Church Welfare Committee, Paul C. Child. President Child was a student of the scriptures. He had been my stake president during my Aaronic Priesthood years. Now we were together as conference visitors.

When it was his opportunity to participate in the priesthood leadership session, President Child picked up the Doctrine and Covenants and left the pulpit to stand among the priesthood to whom he was directing his message. He turned to section 18 and began to read:

"Remember the worth of souls is great in the sight of God. . . . And if it so be that you should labor all your days in crying repentance unto this people, and bring, save it be one soul unto me, how great shall be your joy with him in the kingdom of my Father!" (D&C 18:10, 15.)

President Child then raised his eyes from the scriptures and asked the priesthood brethren: "What is the worth of a human soul?" He avoided calling on a bishop, stake president, or high councilor for a response. Instead, he selected the president of an elders quorum—a brother who had been a bit drowsy and had missed the significance of the question.

The startled man responded: "Brother Child, could you please repeat the question?" The question was repeated: "What is the worth of a human soul?"

I knew President Child's style. I prayed fervently for

that quorum president. He remained silent for what seemed like an eternity and then declared, "Brother Child, the worth of a human soul is its capacity to become as God."

All present pondered that reply. Brother Child returned to the stand, leaned over to me, and said, "A profound reply!" He proceeded with his message, but I continued to reflect on that inspired response.

The Calling of a Stake President

In the autumn of 1967, a program was established whereby regional representatives of the Council of the Twelve were appointed. Many were stake presidents; hence, it was necessary to reorganize a number of the presidencies of the stakes, particularly in the greater Salt Lake Valley.

One of the presidents to be thus released was Stanford Smith of the Bountiful Stake. I received the appointment to reorganize the stake presidency.

At the quarterly conference, Elder Milton R. Hunter of the First Council of the Seventy and I conducted a series of interviews late into the evening. As we would interview brethren, three names generally came forward by way of nomination.

We were conducting our last interview for the evening with a bishop, who gave me the names of three men. Then he said, "Brother Monson, I've given you the names of the brethren who more than likely would become members of the stake presidency, but there is another man who I feel might be a fine stake president." I asked him who that would be. He said, "My second counselor, Edgar M. Denny."

I did not see a light nor did I hear a supernatural voice, yet I knew that the name that had been spoken was indeed the new stake president.

I conferred with President Stanford Smith, and he felt, likewise, that Brother Denny should have an interview. President Smith telephoned the Denny home, whereupon Sister Denny said, "I'm sorry, President Smith, but my husband is in Florida and won't be back until tomorrow." She then said, "Excuse me just a moment; there's a knock at the door." She returned to the phone. "You'll never believe what I'm about to tell you. My husband has come home a day early. Would you like to speak to him?"

We invited Brother and Sister Denny to come to the office, and he was called to be the president of the Bountiful Stake. The people of the Bountiful Stake knew, as did I and as did the Denny family, that the call of their stake president had been inspired by God.

A Long-Postponed Blessing

&

A few years ago I read an obituary in the daily newspaper noting the passing of a man I had known from my youth. The obituary mentioned his wife and children and gave a brief account of his life. The words that registered on my mind were these: "Marriage later solemnized in the Salt Lake Temple."

Backward, ever backward, my thoughts turned to a special day when, in the temple of God, I performed that sacred sealing. Jack was a good man, a generous man. However, it remained the privilege and opportunity of a loving, patient, and understanding wife to quicken within him the desire to live a better life and walk the higher road.

The sealing room of the temple was a scene of tranquility. The cares of the outside world had been temporarily discarded. The quiet and peace of the house of the Lord filled the heart of each one assembled in the room.

I knew that this particular couple had been married for eighteen years before coming to the temple. I turned to the husband and asked, "Jack, who is responsible for bringing this glorious event to fulfillment?" He smiled and silently pointed to his precious wife, who sat by his side. I seemed to sense that this lovely woman was never more proud of her husband than at that particular moment. Jack then directed my attention to one of the brethren serving as a witness to this ceremony and acknowledged the great influence for good that he had had upon his life.

As the three beautiful children were sealed to their parents, I could not help noticing the tears that welled up in the eyes of the teenage daughter and then coursed in little rivulets down her cheeks, finally tumbling upon clasped hands. These were sacred tears, tears of supreme joy, tears that expressed silent but eloquent gratitude of a tender heart too full to speak.

I found myself thinking, "Oh, that such men and women would not wait eighteen long years to receive this priceless blessing."

Faith in Nuku'alofa

❦

In the spring of 1968, at the time the Nuku'alofa Stake was formed by Elder Howard W. Hunter and me, I had an interesting experience in the ordination of a dear Tongan brother named Mosese Muti. He was called to the high council.

I placed my hands upon his head and ordained him a high priest and set him apart to be a member of the high council. I noted that the blessing had affected his emotions, and I commented about this. Brother Muti said to me, "Brother Monson, many years ago Elder George Albert Smith visited these islands and ordained me an elder. In his blessing he said that I would live to see the day when another apostle would return to our islands and that I would have the privilege of being ordained a high priest. This day this prophecy has been fulfilled."

During this same visit to Tonga, a woman bade me farewell as Frances and I departed Tonga. She said that two weeks earlier her son had been summoned to her bedside, inasmuch as her life was despaired of. In his blessing, he promised his mother that she would live to see the creation of the first stake in Tonga. Her health had been miraculously restored. The blessing had been fulfilled.

A Daughter's Testimony

Long ago I received a glimpse of eternity and what it means to be sealed in the temple of God. I received a telephone call from a lovely woman, now a widow. She and her husband had been members of the Temple View Stake when I lived there. She called to say that her precious daughter, in the prime of life, had passed away.

The night before the funeral, I went to the mortuary, where I saw a host of friends and family. At one end of the room was the open casket. Within the casket I saw the body of this beautiful, sweet mother and devoted wife, the daughter of my friend. At the side of the casket stood the husband to whom she had been sealed, along with their children, the oldest to the youngest. Before I could say a word, a tiny girl, the first one in the line, looked up and said, "I know who you are. You are Brother Monson." Then, with her hand in mine, she took me to the open casket and said, "Isn't she pretty? She's my mommy." Tears began to blur my vision. She looked up again and said, "Don't cry, Brother Monson. Look at me; I'm not crying. My mommy taught me about the temple and eternity and promised me we would be together again, and my mommy always told the truth."

I stooped down to where I could look at her and said, "Little one, you will indeed be with your mommy again, for you are a family forever." The truth, taught by a mother, had found lodgment in the heart of a child.

An Inscription in a Book

Some years ago I attended a stake conference in the southern part of the United States where Elder Delbert L. Stapley of the Council of the Twelve had served as a missionary in his youth. After the conference concluded, a sister came forward and opened for my view a rather old copy of the Book of Mormon. She asked, "Do you know the man who inscribed this book when he was a missionary and presented it to my grandparents?"

I looked at the signature, immediately recognized its authenticity, and replied, "Yes. I serve with Elder Stapley."

She asked, "Would you please take this book to Elder Stapley with our love? Tell him that his testimony and this book guided my entire family to become members of the Church."

I wholeheartedly consented to her request. I waited for an appropriate opportunity and then went to Elder Stapley's office, told him of my experience, and handed him the copy of the Book of Mormon he had presented many years before. He read the inscription he had written on the title page of the book and saw his name; then tears came to his eyes. Teaching through testimony had brought to him indescribable joy and profound gratitude.

EXAMPLE OF THE BELIEVERS

Be thou an example of the believers,
in word, in conversation, in spirit,
in faith, in purity.

1 TIMOTHY 4:12

A Beloved Teacher

§

It was my experience as a small boy to come under the influence of a great teacher, Lucy Gertsch. We met for the first time on a Sunday morning. She accompanied the Sunday School superintendent into the classroom and was presented to us as a teacher who actually requested the opportunity to teach us. We learned that she had been a missionary and loved young people.

Lucy Gertsch was beautiful, soft-spoken, and interested in us. She asked each class member to introduce himself or herself, and then she asked questions that gave her an understanding and insight into the background of each boy, each girl. She told us of her childhood in Midway, Utah; and as she described that beautiful valley, she made its beauty live, and we desired to visit the green fields and clear streams she loved so much. She never raised her voice. Somehow rudeness and boisterousness were incompatible with the beauty of her lessons. She taught us that the present is here and that we must live in it. She made the scriptures actually come to life. We became personally acquainted with Samuel, David, Jacob, Nephi, and the Lord Jesus Christ. Our gospel scholarship grew. Our deportment improved. Our love for Lucy knew no bounds.

In our Sunday School class, she taught us concerning the creation of the world, the fall of Adam, the atoning sacrifice of Jesus. She brought to her classroom as honored guests Moses, Joshua, Peter, Thomas, Paul, and even Christ. Though we did not see them, we learned to love, honor, and emulate them.

Never was her teaching so dynamic nor its impact more

everlasting than one Sunday morning when she sadly announced to us the passing of a classmate's mother. We had missed Billy that morning but knew not the reason for his absence. The lesson featured the theme "It is more blessed to give than to receive." Midway through the lesson, our teacher closed the manual and opened our eyes and our ears and our hearts to the glory of God. She asked, "How much money do we have in our class party fund?" Depression days prompted a proud answer: "Four dollars and seventy-five cents." Then ever so gently she suggested: "Billy's family is hard-pressed and grief-stricken. What would you think of the possibility of visiting the family members this morning and giving them your fund?"

Ever shall I remember the tiny band walking those three city blocks, entering Billy's home, greeting him and his brother, sisters, and father. Noticeably absent was his mother. Always I shall treasure the tears that glistened in the eyes of all as the white envelope containing our precious party fund passed from the delicate hand of our teacher to the needy hand of a grief-stricken father. We fairly skipped back to the chapel. Our hearts were lighter than they had ever been, our joy more full, our understanding more profound. A God-inspired teacher had taught her boys and girls an eternal lesson of divine truth. "It is more blessed to give than to receive."

The years have flown. The old chapel is gone, a victim of industrialization. The boys and girls who learned, who laughed, who grew under the direction of that inspired teacher of truth have never forgotten her love or her lessons.

A Father's Hands

During the period of the Great Depression I was a small boy. Fortunate were those men who had work. Jobs were few, hours long, pay scant.

On our street was a father who, though old in years, supported with the labor of his hands his rather large family of girls. His firm was known as the Spring Canyon Coal Company. It consisted of one old truck, a pile of coal, one shovel, one man, and his own two hands.

From early morning to late evening he struggled to survive. Yet during the monthly fast and testimony meeting, I specifically remember him expressing his thanks to the Lord for his family, for his work, and for his testimony. The fingers of those rough, red, chapped hands turned white as they gripped the back of the bench on which I sat as Brother James Farrell bore witness of a boy, even Joseph Smith, who, in a grove of trees near Palmyra, New York, knelt in prayer and beheld the heavenly vision of God the Father and Jesus Christ the Son. The memory of those hands serve to remind me of Brother Farrell's abiding faith, his honest conviction, and his testimony of truth.

Kindness to a Stranger

Junius Burt, a longtime worker in the Salt Lake City Streets Department, related a touching and inspirational experience. He said that many years ago, on a cold winter morning, the street cleaning crew of which he was a member was removing large chunks of ice from the street gutters. The regular crew was assisted by temporary laborers who desperately needed the work. One such man wore only a lightweight sweater and was suffering from the cold.

A slender man with a well-groomed beard stopped by the crew and said to the worker, "You need more than that sweater on a morning like this. Where is your coat?"

The man replied that he had no coat to wear.

The visitor then removed his own overcoat, handed it to the man, and said, "This coat is yours. It is heavy wool and will keep you warm. I just work across the street."

The street was South Temple. The Good Samaritan who walked into the Church Administration Building to his daily work and without his coat was President George Albert Smith of The Church of Jesus Christ of Latter-day Saints. His selfless act of generosity revealed his tender heart.

Sacrament Prayers

§

The privilege to magnify our callings may come without announcement or fanfare. When I was a deacon, I recall sitting on the front row of benches in the chapel, along with the other deacons, as the priests prepared to bless the sacrament. One of the priests, whose name was Leland, had a "golden" voice. When he offered the prayer at the sacrament table, the words were clearly pronounced and beautifully spoken. Many would compliment him when the meeting concluded. I think he became a bit proud.

Another priest, named John, sat with Leland of the golden voice one day. John had a hearing impairment and an accompanying speech problem. His words were somewhat difficult to understand. Often we deacons would snicker a bit when John prayed. How we dared to do so is difficult to understand, for John had fists like bear paws and could have silenced us simply by doubling up those fists.

On one particular Sunday, the bread was broken, the hymn was sung. All bowed their heads as Leland prepared to pray. We heard no words spoken. The silence seemed eternal. I opened my eyes and saw Leland looking frantically for the small card on which the words of the prayer were printed. It was nowhere to be found. Others began to open their eyes and raise their heads in wondering. Just then, John, with the hearing and speaking problems, reached forth with one of his mighty hands and gently guided Leland back to the bench. Then John knelt down and, from memory, spoke the words of that familiar prayer: "O God, the Eternal Father, we ask thee in the name of thy

Son, Jesus Christ, to bless and sanctify this bread to the souls of all those who partake of it." (Moroni 4:3.) He also blessed the water that morning. He never missed a word.

As we left the chapel that day, Leland said to John, "I thank you from the bottom of my heart for rescuing me today."

John responded, "We are both priests in the same quorum doing our duty." This priest who magnified his calling had changed lives, altered perspectives, and taught an everlasting lesson: Whom God calls, God qualifies.

The Missing Baseballs

§.

When I was a deacon, I loved baseball; in fact, I still do. I had a fielder's glove inscribed with the name "Mel Ott." He was the Dale Murphy of my day.

My friends and I would play ball in a small alleyway behind the houses where we lived. The quarters were cramped but all right, provided you hit straight away to center field. However, if you hit the ball to the right of center, disaster was at the door. Here lived Mrs. Shinas, who would watch us play, and, as soon as the ball rolled to her porch, her English setter dog would retrieve the ball and present it to her as she opened the door. Into her house she would return and add the ball to the many she had previously confiscated.

Mrs. Shinas was our nemesis, the destroyer of our fun—even the bane of our existence. None of us had a good word for her. The windows of her house received more special soap treatment on Halloween than did any other. None of us would speak to her, and she never spoke to us. She was hampered by a stiff leg, which impaired her walking and must have caused her great pain. She and her husband had no children, lived secluded lives, and rarely came out of their house.

This private war continued for some time—perhaps two years—and then an inspired thaw melted the ice of winter and brought a springtime of good feelings to the stalemate. One night as I performed my daily task of hand-watering our front lawn, holding the nozzle of the hose in hand as was the style at that time, I noticed that Mrs. Shinas's lawn was dry and turning brown. I honestly don't know what came over me, but I took a few more minutes and, with our hose, watered her lawn. This I did each night, and when autumn came, I hosed her lawn free of leaves as I did ours and stacked the leaves in piles at the street's edge to be burned or gathered. During the entire summer I had not seen Mrs. Shinas. We had long since given up playing ball in the alley. We had run out of baseballs and had no money to buy more.

Then early one evening her front door opened, and Mrs. Shinas beckoned for me to jump the small fence and come to her front porch. This I did, and as I approached her, she invited me into her living room, where I was asked to sit in a comfortable chair.

Mrs. Shinas went to the kitchen and returned with a large box filled with baseballs and softballs, representing several seasons of her confiscation efforts. The filled box was presented to me; however, the treasure was not to be found in the gift, but rather in her voice. I saw for the first time a smile come across the face of Mrs. Shinas, and she said, "Tommy, I want you to have these baseballs, and I want to thank you for being kind to me." I expressed my own gratitude to her and walked from her home a better boy than when I entered. No longer were we enemies. Now we were friends. The Golden Rule had again succeeded.

Boot Camp

Navy boot camp was not an easy experience for me, nor for anyone who endured it. For the first three weeks, one felt as though the Navy was trying to kill rather than train him.

I shall ever remember the first Sunday at the Naval Training Center, San Diego. The chief petty officer said to us, "Today everybody goes to church." We then lined up in formation on the drill ground.

The petty officer shouted, "All of you who are Catholics—you meet in Camp Decatur. Forward, march!" And a large number marched out.

He then said, "All of you who are of the Jewish faith— you meet in Camp Henry. Forward, march!" And a smaller contingent moved out.

Then he said, "The rest of you Protestants meet in the theaters at Camp Farragut. Forward, march! And don't come back until two o'clock."

There flashed through my mind the thought, "Monson, you're not a Catholic. Monson, you're not a Jew. Monson, you're not a Protestant." I elected to stand fast. It seemed as though hundreds of men marched by me.

I then heard the words, the sweetest that the petty officer ever uttered in my presence, "And what do you fellows call yourselves?" He used the plural. This was the first time I knew that anyone else was standing behind me on that drill ground.

In unison we said, "We're Mormons."

He scratched his head in an expression of puzzlement and said, "Well, go find somewhere to meet."

Boot Camp

We marched away. One could almost count cadence to the rhyme learned in Primary:

> Dare to be a Mormon;
> Dare to stand alone;
> Dare to have a purpose firm;
> And dare to make it known.

Yellow Canaries with Gray on Their Wings

When I was a young man serving as the bishop of a large ward in Salt Lake City, one evening, at a late hour, my telephone rang. I heard a voice say, "Bishop Monson, this is the hospital calling. Kathleen McKee, a member of your congregation, has just passed away. Our records reveal that she had no next of kin, but your name is listed as the one to be notified in the event of her death. Could you come to the hospital right away?"

Upon arriving there, I was presented with a sealed envelope that contained a key to the modest apartment in which Kathleen McKee had lived. A childless widow seventy-three years of age, she had enjoyed but few of life's luxuries and possessed scarcely sufficient of its necessities. In the twilight of her life, she had become a member of The Church of Jesus Christ of Latter-day Saints. Being a quiet and overly reserved person, little was known about her.

That same night I entered her tidy basement apartment, turned on the light switch, and in a moment discovered a letter written ever so meticulously in Kathleen McKee's own hand. It rested face up on a small table and read:

> Bishop Monson,
>
> I think I shall not return from the hospital. In the dresser drawer is a small insurance policy that will cover funeral expenses. The furniture may be given to my neighbors.
>
> In the kitchen are my three precious canaries. Two of them are beautiful, yellow-gold in color,

and are perfectly marked. On their cages I have noted the names of friends to whom they are to be given. In the third cage is "Billie." He is my favorite. Billie looks a bit scrubby, and his yellow hue is marred by gray on his wings. Will you and your family make a home for him? He isn't the prettiest, but his song is the best.

She had also left two Alka Seltzer bottles filled with quarters, and this message: "Bishop, here is my fast offering. I am square with the Lord." A spirit of peace filled that apartment. A silent sermon had been delivered.

In the days that followed, I learned much more about Kathleen McKee. She had befriended many neighbors in need. She had given cheer and comfort almost daily to a physically handicapped person who lived down the street. Indeed, she had brightened each life she touched.

Kathleen McKee was much like "Billie," her prized yellow canary with gray on its wings. She was not blessed with beauty, gifted with poise, or honored by posterity. Yet her song helped others to more willingly bear their burdens and more ably shoulder their tasks.

A Blind Man's Song

Long years ago I was summoned to the LDS Hospital in Salt Lake City to the bedside of a man who was an inactive member of the Church and who had many weaknesses, a man who was in danger of dying. As I walked to the hospital ward, I noted the sign on the doorway, "Intensive care. Enter only upon permission of the nurse." I sought the required permission, then went to the bedside of this good man.

The great machines of medical science were by his side, mechanically taking over when his heart would falter. An oxygen mask covered his face. He turned his face toward me, but there was no glimmer of recognition in his eyes, for the man in whose presence I stood was blind and had been for many years. Yet as he heard my voice and thought back on more pleasant times, tears began to stream from those sightless eyes, and he asked a blessing from one who held the priesthood of God.

At the conclusion of that blessing, I recalled how this man had been blessed with a beautiful voice. While he was not a regular attender at church, he would come— particularly on Mother's Day—and sing the beautiful number "That Wonderful Mother of Mine" and other songs honoring mothers. No person who ever heard him sing left without a greater appreciation for his own mother, which resulted in his honoring her and all womanhood. Similarly, this man would participate in Christmas programs and would sing "The Holy City." No person who heard him sing this song came away without dedicating his life to better serving the Lord and keeping Christmas, rather than spending Christmas.

The thought came into my heart that here was a man who, in his own humble way, had used the talent God had given him to bring joy and happiness into the lives of others and inspired them to greater heights.

A Son's First Blessing

ꙮ

Each year it has been my custom near Christmas time to take to the remaining widows from the roster of the old Sixth-Seventh Ward, where I served as bishop long years ago, a plump roasting chicken and a Christmas greeting. Inevitably, these dear sisters ask for a blessing.

My children would vie for the opportunity to go with me. In December of 1970, my son Tom and I paid a visit to several of the homes. At Elizabeth Keachie's home, she sought a blessing, that she might have added health and strength.

I turned to Tom, inasmuch as just a few weeks before I had had the privilege of ordaining him an elder. I asked him if he would anoint, and then I would seal the anointing.

Thus, father and son participated in that son's first ordinance in the Melchizedek Priesthood. It was a day I shall never forget. It was a setting I shall ever remember.

Becoming a Deacon

As our youngest son, Clark, was approaching his twelfth birthday, he and I were leaving the Church Administration Building when President Harold B. Lee approached and greeted us. I mentioned that Clark would soon be twelve, whereupon President Lee turned to him and asked, "What happens to you when you turn twelve?"

This was one of those times when a father prays that a son will be inspired to give a proper response. Clark, without hesitation, said to President Lee, "I will be ordained a deacon!"

The answer was the one President Lee had sought. He then counseled our son, "Remember, it is a great blessing to hold the priesthood."

More than a Tenth

&

When I was president of the Canadian Mission in Eastern Canada, Brother Gustav Wacker was president of the Kingston Branch. He was from the old country and spoke English with a thick accent. He never owned or drove a car. He plied the trade of a barber. He made but little money cutting hair near an army base at Kingston.

How he loved the missionaries! The highlight of his day would be when he had the privilege to cut the hair of a missionary. Never would there be a charge. When they would make a feeble attempt to pay him, he would say, "Oh no; it is a joy to cut the hair of a servant of the Lord." Indeed, he would reach deep into his pockets and give the missionaries all of his tips for the day. If it was raining, as it often did in Kingston, President Wacker would call a taxi and send the missionaries to their apartment by cab, while he himself at day's end would lock the small shop and walk home alone in the driving rain.

I first met Gustav Wacker when I noticed that his tithing was far in excess of that expected from his potential income. My efforts to explain to him that the Lord required no more than a tenth fell on attentive but unconvinced ears. He simply responded that he loved to pay all he could to the Lord. It amounted to about a third of his income. His dear wife felt exactly as he did. Their unique manner of tithing payment continued.

Gustav and Margarete Wacker established a home that was a heaven. They were not blessed with children, but mothered and fathered the young missionaries who loved to visit them. Men of learning, men of experience sought out this humble, unlettered man of God and counted themselves fortunate if they could spend an hour with him. His appearance was ordinary, his English was halting and somewhat difficult to understand, his home was unpretentious. He didn't own a car or a television; he wrote no books and preached no polished sermons and did none of the things to which the world usually pays attention. Yet the faithful beat a path to his door. Why? Because they wished to drink at his "fountain of truth." Not so much what he said as what he did; not the substance of the sermons he preached but the strength of the life he led. He had the glow of goodness and the radiance of righteousness. His strength came from obedience.

Did our Heavenly Father honor such obedience, such abiding faith? The branch prospered. The membership outgrew the rented Slovakian Hall where they met, and they moved into a modern and lovely chapel of their own to which they had contributed their share and more, that it might grace the city of Kingston.

President and Sister Wacker had their prayers answered by serving a proselyting mission to their native Germany and later a temple mission to the beautiful temple in Washington, D.C. Then in 1983, his mission in mortality concluded, Gustav Wacker peacefully passed away while being held in the loving arms of his eternal companion, dressed in his white temple suit, there in the Washington Temple.

Gustav Wacker did not lay up for himself treasures on earth; rather, he laid up for himself treasures in heaven.

Service from a Wheelchair

&

When the late Boyd Hatch of Salt Lake City was deprived of the use of his legs and was faced with a lifetime in a wheelchair, he could well have looked inward and, through sorrow for self, existed rather than lived. However, Brother Hatch looked not inward, but outward into the lives of others and upward into God's own heaven; and the star of inspiration guided him not to one opportunity but to literally hundreds.

Brother Hatch organized Scout troops of handicapped boys. He taught them camping. He taught them cooking. He taught them basketball. He taught them faith. Some boys were downhearted and filled with self-pity and despair. To them he handed the torch of hope. Before them was his own personal example of struggle and accomplishment. With a courage that we shall never fully know or understand, these boys of many faiths overcame insurmountable odds and found themselves anew.

Through it all, Boyd Hatch experienced the profound joy of serving others.

Service during Exams

A highly successful business executive in Salt Lake City, a friend of mine, once served as a counselor in his ward bishopric, while at the same time pursuing his master's degree. During the hectic period preceding finals, the bishop told him, "Lynn, I know you are facing a crisis in your schooling pursuits. Let us relieve you of your meeting schedule and some of the details of your assignments during the next two weeks."

Lynn answered, "Bishop, I would ask that rather than relieving me of responsibility, you and the other counselor let me assume additional duties. I want to go to the Lord and ask His help by right, not by grace."

He never slackened. He graduated among the highest in his class.

Honesty and a Broken Film

While I was visiting in the distant land of New Zealand years ago, we were showing a film to a group of missionaries. Operating the projector was Elder Dick Nemelka, who had been an all-America basketball star.

During the course of showing the movie, the film was broken. The sound stopped and the lights went on. The elder went about his task of applying a quick splice so the movie could continue. Someone reached over and whispered to him, "Did the film break?" He replied, "No, the film didn't break—I broke it."

No performance on the basketball court ever marked him more as an all-American than did his basic honesty, demonstrated so naturally that night.

White Handkerchiefs

In May of 1967, I had the opportunity to deliver a commencement address to a graduating class. I had gone to the home of President Hugh B. Brown so that we might drive together to the university, where he was to conduct the exercises and I was to speak.

As President Brown entered my car, he said, "Wait a moment." He looked toward the large bay window of his lovely home, and then I realized what he was looking for. The curtain parted, and I saw Sister Zina Brown, his beloved companion of well over fifty years, at the window, propped up in a wheelchair, waving a little white handkerchief. President Brown took from his inside coat pocket a white handkerchief, which he waved to her in return. Then, with a smile, he said to me, "We can go."

As we drove, I asked President Brown to tell me about the white handkerchiefs. He related to me the following incident: "The first day after Sister Brown and I were married, as I went to work I heard a tap at the window, and there was Zina, waving a white handkerchief. I found my handkerchief and waved in reply. From that day until this, I have never left my home without that little exchange between my wife and me. It is a symbol of our love one for another. It is an indication to one another that all will be well until we are again together at eventide." I thought, Perhaps this tender practice helps to account for their long and happy marriage.

A Love of the Scriptures

§♣

Many years ago I received an invitation to meet with President J. Reuben Clark, Jr., a counselor in the First Presidency, a statesman of towering stature, and a scholar of international renown. My profession then was in the field of printing and publishing. President Clark made me welcome in his office and then produced from his old roll-top desk a large sheaf of meticulous, handwritten notes on eight-and-a-half-by-fourteen-inch canary-colored sheets. Many of the notes had been made when he was a law student long years before. He proceeded to outline for me his goal of producing a harmony of the Gospels. This goal was achieved with his monumental work, *Our Lord of the Gospels*. Many years later I still treasure my personally inscribed, leather-bound copy of this classic treatment of the life and teachings of Jesus of Nazareth.

I asked President Clark during one of our many conversations, "Which of the Gospels do you like best?" His answer: "Brother Monson, I love each of the Gospels."

Years later as I perused the pages of *Our Lord of the Gospels* and paused at the section entitled "The Miracles of Jesus," I remembered as though it were yesterday President Clark asking me to read to him several of these accounts while he sat back in his large leather chair and listened. He asked me to read aloud the account found in Luke concerning the man filled with leprosy. Then he asked that I continue reading from Luke concerning the man afflicted with palsy and the enterprising manner in which he was presented to the attention of the Lord, who healed him. President Clark removed from his pocket a

233

handkerchief and wiped the tears from his eyes. He commented, "As we grow older, tears come more frequently." After a few words of good-bye, I departed from his office, leaving him alone with his thoughts and his tears.

Late one evening I delivered some press proofs to his office in his home in Salt Lake City. President Clark was reading from Ecclesiastes, and he was in a quiet and reflective mood. He sat back from his large desk, which was stacked with books and papers. He held the scriptures in his hand, lifted his eyes from the printed page, and read aloud to me: "Let us hear the conclusion of the whole matter: Fear God, and keep his commandments: for this is the whole duty of man." (Ecclesiastes 12:13.) He exclaimed, "A treasured truth! A profound philosophy!"

What a blessing was mine to learn daily at the feet of such a master teacher and a principal architect of the welfare program. Knowing that I was a newly appointed bishop presiding over a challenging ward, he emphasized the need for me to know my people, to understand their circumstances, and to minister to their needs.

One day he recounted the Savior's raising from the dead the son of the widow of Nain, as recorded in the Gospel of Luke. When President Clark closed the Bible, I noticed that he was weeping. In a quiet voice, he said, "Tom, be kind to the widow and look after the poor."

On another occasion he said: "You do not find truth groveling through error. You find truth by seeking truth."

Through the years these conversations have remained bright in my memory.

A Bishop's Wife

§⚬

As a member of the Council of the Twelve, on October 27, 1974, during a visit to Omaha Nebraska Stake, I was assigned to dedicate a building at Council Bluffs, Iowa. Upon my arrival in Nebraska, I discovered there was also a building in Omaha that needed to be dedicated. I felt impressed to suggest that the stake president dedicate the larger one in Omaha, and I would go out to the smaller unit and dedicate that building.

It turned out to be a sweet experience for me. A touching scene occurred when the former bishop's wife, Sister Wiley, who was dying of cancer, was brought from the hospital by ambulance to the building and placed on a hospital bed on the stage at the rear of the building, where she had a commanding view of all of the proceedings. Her husband, who had done so much work in directing the fundraising for the building, was one of the speakers.

I was touched by the fact that her little grandchildren knelt at the side of the bed and held her hand in theirs. She was particularly pleased to see and hear her husband as he delivered a beautiful message on the program. I felt impressed to direct my remarks to the plan of salvation, and to pay tribute to this good woman's support of her husband.

Following the meeting I went to the stage and bade Sister Wiley a tender farewell as she was bundled up and placed in the ambulance for her return trip to the hospital, where she passed away soon afterward. As I returned to Salt Lake City, I uttered a silent prayer of gratitude for the prompting to dedicate the Council Bluffs Ward building.

Music Hallowed by Sacrifice

During a regional conference in England, we addressed a packed audience in Leeds, the city whence came my father's mother. The conducting officer stood and said, "Our director has postponed major surgery for two weeks so that she might lead this chorus. Our organist is presenting his final performance at the organ, as Parkinson's disease has rendered his fingers crippled." As he made those comments in that hall, every heart seemed to be inclined toward the Master, the Stranger of Galilee, who made lame beggars walk and blind men see.

The chorus sang as no chorus has ever before sung in honor of its director, to show their faith and their devotion to her. I heard the organ music rendered by those crippled hands, as a man performed far beyond his ability. At the conclusion, the choir sang the "Hallelujah Chorus" from Handel's *Messiah*. We were in the presence of the Spirit of the Lord, and hearts were touched.

Sunbeam Road

&

Many years ago I visited the Jacksonville Florida Stake, where I learned that the patriarch of the stake, James R. Boone, father of fourteen upstanding and stalwart children, was ill. All through the two sessions of the conference on Sunday, I felt the impression that I should visit James Boone. I had heard his name mentioned as one of the real Church pioneers in the Florida area.

Following that impression, at the conclusion of conference I was driven to the home of Brother Boone. As I arrived at his residence, I did not see a large two-story or three-story structure. I saw a small, humble farm home situated about forty feet from the front gate. There was not a blade of grass growing, but I saw a couple of pigs and some chickens and dogs and a cat or two adorning the front yard. They were waiting for me, it seemed.

Sister Boone, who was serving as the stake Relief Society president, opened the door, and I was escorted into their small home. There was a warm, friendly spirit there. One could tell he was in the presence of those who had strong testimonies.

Brother Boone was lying in the bedroom resting and recuperating from an illness. As I went into this marvelous patriarch's room, I could not help but notice that his library was by his bedside in bookcases made from wooden orange crates. The books, representing the major publications of the Church, were stacked vertically in the crates, and nearest him were the Standard Works of the Church. As I looked upon this wonderful man, a leader in the Church in that area, I thought to myself, our Heavenly

Father has been good to him. He has not blessed him with material things, but He blessed him with a posterity that has done honor to him all through the years.

As I left the Boone home, I noted the address on the mailbox: 3983 Sunbeam. I thought it rather appropriate.

Brother Boone passed away December 4, 1987. His great desire was to have one hundred grandchildren born while he lived in mortality. His wish was granted to him. His one-hundredth grandchild was born on the day that Brother Boone died.

Estonian Saints

When I was president of the Canadian Mission, one of our fine district presidents, Hans Peets, was from Estonia, as was his wife, and I would occasionally speak to them about Estonia. Later, as a member of the Council of the Twelve, I had the privilege of ordaining Brother Peets a patriarch, and many years later he served as a counselor in the first Toronto Temple presidency.

On one occasion early in my service in the Council of the Twelve, I was attending a stake conference in Sydney, Australia. During the morning session, I noticed a man in a wheelchair occupying the center aisle directly in front of me. Somehow I knew I had to talk to him. Right after the session ended, I left the stand and approached him. I said to him, "I feel I need to know your name and to speak to you."

His reply was interesting. He said, "My name is Hugo Orro, and I'm the only baptized Estonian in the Church."

I said to him, "I know of another: Hans Peets from Montreal, Canada." I also mentioned other Estonian members I knew: Endel Terri, a patriarch in London, Ontario, Canada, and his wife, as well as Olav Taim, who lived in South Africa.

We visited for a few minutes, and then Brother Orro left to return home. When he came back to the afternoon session, he called me over to him and showed me an old picture of a Scout troop, the picture having been taken in Tallinn, the capital of Estonia, about 1937. He pointed to the picture and said, "Here am I, Hugo Orro." Then he moved his finger and said, "And here is Hans Peets." Two boys in the same Scout troop in Estonia found freedom and the Church, one in Canada and another in Australia.

Those two wonderful Estonian men, now high priests, wrote to each other and a great friendship resulted.

Inspiration to Announce a Speaker

On Saturday, August 29, 1987, I was attending the dedication of the Frankfurt Temple. Just prior to the Dutch session, I handed a note to Elder Carlos E. Asay asking him whether or not Peter Mourik, an outstanding Dutch member of the Church, would be in attendance at the meeting. Elder Asay passed a note back indicating that Brother Mourik was not in the session but that, inasmuch as he was serving in the Servicemen's Stake, he would attend the following day with the members of that stake.

Despite the word that he wouldn't be in this particular session, I had a distinct impression to call upon Brother Mourik to speak to the assembled throng, so I stood and announced him as the first speaker. Elder Asay later told me that he was astounded with the announcement and wondered if I had been able to read his response to me.

Just as I finished announcing his name, Brother Mourik entered the Celestial Room and gave a most inspiring message to the assembled Saints, who were from Holland and Belgium.

I later learned how Brother Mourik came to be in the meeting. He had been attending stake priesthood meeting for the Servicemen's Stake and, following the meeting, was visiting with Elder Thomas Hawkes, regional representative. Brother Mourik said that all of a sudden he had a strong, undeniable impression that he must go to the Frankfurt Temple. He felt a great urgency to go immediately. Since his wife had his car, he asked Elder Hawkes to drive him—quickly. Elder Hawkes asked, "Why do you need to go to the temple?"

Brother Mourik replied, "I don't know. I just know I have to get there."

Off they flew in Brother Hawkes's car. Brother Mourik hurried into the temple just in time to see me on the hall monitor and hear me say, "Our next speaker will be Peter Mourik."

This event will serve as a spiritual bond between Brother Mourik and me always.

A Memorable Temple Contribution

At the groundbreaking of the Toronto Temple, we heard a lovely account regarding a young lad from the Cornwall Ward, Jacob Fortin. Jacob was ten years old and had the spirit of temple work. When it was announced that a temple would be built in Toronto for all of the Saints of the northeastern part of the U.S. and the eastern part of Canada, little Jacob began to pencil in on his weekly tithing donation slip a few pennies, and he just put "Temple" as the designated fund. Consequently, every week Jacob developed more and more of the spirit of the temple.

Jacob's grandmother, for his birthday, gave him a new twenty-dollar bill. Jacob had been planning all year what he might do with his birthday money. But all of that changed, for he had received the spirit of temple work. Without telling his mother or his father or anyone else, he slipped the entire twenty dollars in the donation envelope and marked it for the temple fund.

Jacob's father was a member of the bishopric, and he was going through the contributions that day to make an accounting of them. There he saw the contribution from his own son. Tears came to his eyes as he realized that here was a ten-year-old boy who had caught the majesty of the spirit of temple work. He later said to Jacob, "Son, what prompted you to contribute the entire twenty dollars, which is a large sum for you, to the building of the House of the Lord?"

Jacob's answer was classic. He said, "I love my Heavenly Father, and I want His house to be beautiful."

ON THE LIGHTER SIDE

*A merry heart
maketh a cheerful countenance.*

PROVERBS 15:13

An Unexpected Donation

During my Primary years, the Primary Children's Hospital in Salt Lake City was located in a remodeled house on North Temple Street, but a new hospital was soon to be constructed on the Avenues. Each Wednesday afternoon in Primary, we would talk about the future Primary Children's Hospital, where little children could be cared for and where skilled physicians could mend broken limbs and ease the effects of sickness.

In our ward we had a cardboard replica of the planned new hospital. It formed a bank with a little slot in the top of it. Each Wednesday we would sing and march to the tune, "Give, said the little stream, Give, oh! give, give, oh! give. Give, said the little stream, As it hurried down the hill." To its cadence we would walk by the bank and put our pennies in it. I recall sitting next to a dear friend of mine and saying, "Jack, I've got a good idea. I have in my pocket a dime and a penny. When we march by and put that penny in the little bank, let's just march right out the front door. We won't go to class at all, but I'll take you over to the Hatch Dairy, and with my dime we'll buy two of those delicious five-cent fudgesicles."

Jack said, "Let's see the dime." He was doubting. Financial depression did that to boys.

I reached in my pocket, produced the dime, and then carefully returned it to its safe place. Suddenly we heard the strains of the music and stood and marched by the little bank as we sang "Give, said the little stream."

I reached in my pocket and dropped my coin in the bank, walked out the front door with Jack, and headed for the Hatch Dairy. Just then he said, "Let's see the dime again." I reached into my pocket to show him the dime and produced the penny! The dime had gone to the Primary Children's Hospital.

As a disappointed boy, I walked back and put the penny also in the bank. For a long while I felt that I, perhaps, had the most substantial investment in the new Primary Children's Hospital—more so than any other boy.

Cowboy or Banker?

When I was about nine years old and attending elementary school in Salt Lake City, all of the youth in the city's schools were asked to fill out a form indicating what we wanted to be when we grew up. The lists were then to be placed in a waterproof metal box and buried beneath a new flagpole that would grace the entrance to the City and County Building grounds. Years later, the box was to be opened and its contents made available.

As I sat with pencil in hand, I thought of the question, What do I want to be when I grow up? Almost without hesitation, I wrote the word *cowboy*. At lunch that day, I reported to my mother my response. I can almost see Mother now as she admonished me, "You get right back to school and change that to banker or lawyer!" I obeyed, and all dreams of being a cowboy vanished forever.

Over thirty-five years later, when I was appointed to serve on the board of a well-known bank, I took a clipping from the newspaper indicating that I was a director of the bank, along with my diploma from the University of Utah, to my mother and father's home. I said, "Mother, all of my life I can remember your telling me that you had three ambitions for me: (1) that I would be a banker—here's a clipping indicating I have fulfilled that ambition; (2) that I would graduate from the university—here's my diploma; (3) that I could play the piano." I stepped over to her piano and rendered "Chopsticks." My mother, half smiling and half crying, thanked me, but then she added, "With more practice, you could do better at the piano." Somehow mothers seem to instinctively know just what to say on such occasions.

Front Row of the Balcony

&

I attended many movies in my boyhood, mostly Westerns. We always liked to sit on the front row of the balcony. But I worry when I see people on the front row of a balcony as I contemplate my experience one Saturday afternoon at the old Victory Theater in Salt Lake City. We hurried as a group of boys to obtain our favorite seats on the front row, but alas, they were occupied by others. We sat on the second row and waited for the feature to change, and change it did.

Then, as boys would do, rather than walking to the edge of the aisle, we thought it would be much more simple just to step over the back of the seat in front of us and take that front row position that had been vacated when the feature changed. We did so in unison. Three out of the four of us accomplished the task without difficulty. The fourth, however, stepped on a seat that was upraised, and as his weight touched the seat, it flipped down, and the spring catapulted him right out of the balcony.

We peered over the edge to see what had happened. Had he struck those straight-backed chairs, he would have been injured; but he was positioned right over the aisle at the precise time that a very large woman was leaving the theater. She never knew what struck her. We hurried downstairs to see how our pal was and observed the ushers carrying the woman into the office. We could hear her mutter, "Where am I? Where am I?" Back we went to the front row of the balcony and watched the second feature. No damage done—but a good lesson learned!

A Lesson in Egg Production

In the stake where I once lived and served, we operated a poultry project. Most of the time it was an efficiently operated project, supplying to the bishop's storehouse countless dozens of fresh eggs and hundreds of pounds of dressed poultry. On a few occasions, however, the experience of being volunteer city farmers provided not only blisters on the hands but also frustration of heart and mind.

For instance, I shall ever remember the time we gathered together the Aaronic Priesthood young men to really give the project a spring cleaning treatment. Our enthusiastic and energetic throng assembled at the project and in a speedy fashion uprooted, gathered, and burned large quantities of weeds and debris. By the light of the glowing bonfires, we ate hot dogs and congratulated ourselves on a job well done. The project was now neat and tidy.

However, there was just one disastrous problem: The noise and the fires had so disturbed the fragile and temperamental population of several thousand laying hens that most of them went into a sudden molt and ceased laying. Thereafter we tolerated a few weeds, so that we might produce more eggs.

"We Want Monson!"

During my basketball years I had the opportunity of sinking the winning basket and of likewise missing what could have been the tying foul shot, but never did I have quite as embarrassing an experience as occurred in the midst of a hectic game.

The lead had alternated back and forth throughout the first half. It was the commencement of the second half. The coach gave me a key play and directed me on the floor to run the play.

As I received the ball, I began to dribble down toward the basket. To my amazement, the opposing forwards and guards opened up and let me through. Even the center stepped aside.

I went up for the lay-up shot, and as the ball left my fingers, I suddenly realized why the opposition had made room for my drive. I was shooting for the wrong basket. Instantly I offered a prayer. It was simple. It was direct. "Dear God, don't let the ball go in."

That basketball rimmed the hoop around and around and then fell out. I heaved a sigh of relief. A cheer came forward from the lovely young women in the cheering section: "We want Monson, we want Monson, we want Monson—out!" The coach obliged.

A Crucial Catch

I know what it is to face disappointment and youthful humiliation. As a boy, I played team softball in elementary and junior high school. Two captains were chosen, and then they, in turn, selected the players they desired on their teams. Of course, the best players were chosen first, then second and third. To be selected fourth or fifth was not too bad, but to be chosen last and relegated to a remote position in the outfield was downright awful. I know. I was there.

How I hoped that the ball would never be hit in my direction, for surely I would drop it, runners would score, and teammates would laugh.

As though it were just yesterday, I remember the moment when all that changed in my life. The game started out as I have described: I was chosen last. I made my sorrowful way to the deep pocket of right field and watched as the other team filled the bases with runners. Two batters then went down on strikes. Suddenly the next batter hit a mighty drive. The ball was coming in my direction. Was it beyond my reach? I raced for the spot where I thought the ball would drop, uttered a silent prayer as I ran, and stretched forth my cupped hands. I surprised myself. I caught the ball! My team won the game.

This one experience bolstered my confidence, inspired my desire to practice, and led me from that last-to-be-chosen place to become a real contributor to the team.

Meeting Frances

My wife, Frances, and I met at a Hello Day dance at the University of Utah when we were freshmen. I can still remember the evening. I went with a girl from my high school, and we were dancing to a tune called "Kentucky." I saw this beautiful girl dance by, and I thought, "There's a girl I want to meet." But she danced away, and I didn't see her again for the rest of the evening and for some time afterward.

Then one day, who should I see standing on the corner of Thirteenth East and Second South but the same girl I saw dancing at our Hello Day dance. I thought, "Do I have the courage? Do I have the faith?" She was with another young woman and a young man with whom I had gone to elementary school. I could not remember his name, but I decided it was now or never. I walked up to him and said, "Hello, old friend."

He said, "Hello, old friend. I don't remember your name."

I said, "You don't?" I gave him my name. Then he introduced me to Frances and the other young woman, and we rode downtown on the streetcar.

That day I made a little note in my student directory to call on Frances Beverly Johnson, and I did. That decision, I believe, was perhaps the most important decision I have ever made. Our marriage took place three and a half years after we met.

A Swedish Name

Frances, my wife, is only one generation away from Scandinavia. Her parents were both born in Sweden—her mother in Eskilstuna and her father at Smedjebacken at Dalarna. Although her name was Johnson, I didn't really know she was Swedish when I first met her. However, I soon found out about her Swedish ancestry.

I was shy as I called at her home the first time and met her parents. Her father said to me when he heard my name, "Monson—that's a Swedish name!"

I replied, "Yes, sir."

He said, "Very good." And then he added, "Just a moment," and he went to a little bureau and brought forth a picture of two missionaries in their top hats. The names of the missionaries were shown at the bottom of the photograph. One name was Elias Monson.

My future father-in-law asked, "Are you related to this man?"

I looked at the name and picture and said, "Why, yes, that's my grandfather's brother."

And then Frances's father began to weep. He said, "He is one of the missionaries who brought the gospel to my mother and father and to all my brothers and sisters and me." Then he put his arms around me, and I knew I had won an advocate.

Creation of the Sixth-Seventh Ward

Let me recount how the Sixth-Seventh Ward in which I lived and served came to have a hyphenated name. In 1922, when the Sixth Ward and the Seventh Ward of the Pioneer Stake in Salt Lake City were faced with a loss of membership due to the industrialization of the west side of the city, it was determined to consolidate the two units.

On the appointed Sunday, the bishop of the Sixth Ward stood at the pulpit for the last time and spoke to his congregation. He said, "At 10:15 we will leave this chapel forever. We will march out of the front doors and, to the accompaniment of the Poulton Brothers Brass Band, will proceed down Third West, then left on Fifth South, moving forward until we enter the doors of the Seventh Ward Chapel and become members of the newly created Sixth-Seventh Ward."

At this same hour, the bishop of the Seventh Ward addressed his congregation, saying, "In just a few minutes the doors of this chapel will swing open as we welcome to this building the members of the Sixth Ward. I have just one word of advice to give you regarding these fine people: Be careful what you say about any of them; they are all related."

The wards were merged, and the work of the Lord moved forward.

Home Teaching in Arbor Ward

Many years ago an interesting experience occurred with respect to home teaching in the Arbor Ward of the Temple View Stake. During a stake priesthood leadership meeting, the stake president ecstatically noted that one ward had 100 percent home teaching. He asked the bishop to come forth and give an explanation. He then made the fatal error of asking the bishop of the ward that had the lowest percentage to come forward and give an accounting.

The first bishop came to the pulpit and for fifteen minutes gave a splendid talk explaining the wonderful organization within his ward. He pointed out that home teachers made their initial visit within the first two weeks of the month. "If this is not accomplished," he said, "then the quorum presidents make the visit within the next ten days of the month. If this is not accomplished, then a member of the bishopric makes the visit. This is how we achieve 100 percent home teaching in our ward."

All this time the other bishop was wondering what he could say. There was silence as he came forward to the pulpit in a less happy mood. He put his large jaw into the microphone and said, "For the last fifteen minutes we have heard how in one ward they have been able to achieve 100 percent home teaching. My assignment is to tell you why in our ward we have achieved much less. I'll be brief. In our ward we are honest!"

The audience laughed. The next month, however, all wards dropped a percentage point or two. Perhaps a lesson had been learned.

Know the Territory

One of the essential requirements in leadership is to "know the territory." When I was a member of the Priesthood Missionary Committee, one of the stakes assigned to me was the Wasatch Stake in Heber City, Utah. I reviewed the report of this stake and was appalled by the relatively few persons serving as stake missionaries. I was newly returned from presiding over the Canadian Mission and carried the natural enthusiasm one does for missionary work. I emphasized to our committee chairman, Elder Spencer W. Kimball, that this stake would soon have more than four stake missionaries. Elder Kimball wisely suggested that I visit the stake and learn the situation and then determine the need for stake missionaries.

In Heber City, meeting with the priesthood leaders, I called at random on the bishop of the Midway Second Ward to report how many brethren from his ward were serving as stake missionaries. Bishop Gertsch reported that there were no stake missionaries serving from his ward. I moved swiftly to make my point and asked, "Bishop, how many nonmembers of the Church do you have living within your ward boundaries?" I was not prepared for his answer. He responded, "We have one nonmember living in the ward, Brother Monson." Not to be outdone, although obviously taken aback, I countered, "And what are you doing to bring that precious nonmember to the waters of baptism?" He said, "He assists in the ward custodial work, and his wife is active as a teacher in Primary. We're making progress."

I had met my match. I simply concluded the matter by saying, "God bless you, Bishop. Keep up the good work."

Coincidence in the Tabernacle

When President David O. McKay extended to me the call to the apostleship, I could feel the Spirit of the Lord within that great leader. He asked that I keep the call confidential, that I reveal the information to no one except my wife, and that I be present in the Tabernacle the next morning when my name would be read.

The following morning I went into the Tabernacle not knowing where to sit. Being a member of the Church Home Teaching Committee, I determined that I would sit among the members of that committee—right in front. As I headed for a seat on the fifth or sixth row in the Tabernacle, I noted a friend of mine by the name of Hugh Smith, who was also a member of the Home Teaching Committee. He motioned for me to sit by him, and as I did so, he said, "I really don't know if you want to sit here or not."

"Why, Brother Smith?" I asked.

He answered, "A strange coincidence: the last two times that a General Authority has been appointed, the fellow was sitting right next to me when his name was read." I couldn't say a thing, but I sat down. In a few moments, the members of the Twelve were sustained and, of course, my name was read. Hugh Smith looked at me and said simply, "Lightning has struck for the third time!"

What's in a Name?

‹a›

Many years ago I received an assignment to visit stake conferences in Australia, that vast continent where drought is an ever-present problem. The Saints in the stakes and missions had written me through their leadership, asking that I join with them in a mighty prayer to our Heavenly Father that moisture would indeed accompany me in my projected visit.

En route to the conference appointments, I noted with some amusement the names of the stake presidents on whom I was to call. The first was President Percy Rivers; the second was William Waters. I called this to the attention of my traveling companion, only to be reminded by him that his name was Harry Brooks. We had a good laugh over this unusual assortment of names.

Upon our arrival at the Sydney International Airport, we were surprised to learn that the name of the house-keeper at the mission home was Sister Rainey.

When we traveled to Brisbane and registered for our motel accommodations, the clerk could not locate the advance reservation. After some difficulty, he responded: "Oh, yes. Here it is. Mr. Thomas S. Monsoon."

Throughout my visit, not a drop of moisture fell from the skies.

A Surprise Avoided

Sometimes rather interesting experiences occur when General Authorities stay in the homes of members during stake conferences. Once when I went to a conference of the Indianapolis Indiana Stake, stake president Philip Low said to me on Saturday, "Would you like to journey eighty miles to Lafayette, where I live, and stay overnight at our home, or would you prefer to stay here in Indianapolis at the home of my counselor?"

I reflected, *Eighty miles each way!*

I then replied to President Low, "I'll stay here at the home of your counselor."

The next morning, the stake president came to the conference and said, "Brother Monson, last evening you made an inspired decision. Our son came home unexpectedly from BYU, tiptoed up the stairs to our bedroom, where you would have been sleeping, opened the door, turned on the light, and yelled, `Surprise!' In my heart I'll never know who would have been more surprised, you or my son!"

An Accidental Signal

One Sunday morning when I had no assignment, I was driving through Provo and decided to go to the Provo Tabernacle to see which stake was holding its conference. It happened to be the Provo Utah West Stake, and my good friend Marion Hinckley was the stake president. He saw me and motioned for me to join him on the stand. I did so and remember sitting directly behind the podium, which, before the tabernacle was remodeled, was very close to the seats on which the stake presidency were seated.

As I sat there, I had my right leg over my left knee, and after a moment or two, I decided it was time to put my left leg over my right knee. I did this just about two minutes after I had arrived. The second counselor, who was speaking at the podium, had been giving his message for only about three minutes. As I shifted my leg, the toe of my shoe accidentally touched the back of his leg. He misunderstood the touch and said rapidly, "In the name of Jesus Christ. Amen."

From that point on, I have tried to keep my feet firmly on the floor when I have been seated on the first row behind the podium anywhere.

"Fresh Courage Take"

After a stake conference in the beautiful land of Japan, a young Japanese convert, perhaps twenty-five or twenty-six years of age, drove my wife and me to the hotel where we were to stay. He was very neat and meticulous in all he did. The car was polished to a brightness seldom seen. He even wore white gloves. I engaged him in conversation, for his English was adequate. As a result of the conversation, I learned that he had a girlfriend who was a member of the Church. I asked him if he loved her. He replied, "Oh, yes, Brother Monson."

My next question was obvious: "Does she love you?"

"Oh, yes, Brother Monson."

I then suggested, "Why don't you ask her to marry you?"

"Oh, I am too shy to ask," he responded.

I then recited the words of the hymn "Come, Come, Ye Saints," with emphasis on the words, "Fresh courage take. Our God will never us forsake."

Some months later I received a lovely letter from my Japanese friend and his sweet wife. They thanked me for my urging and added, "Our favorite hymn is 'Come, Come, Ye Saints.' We took fresh courage. God did not us forsake. Thank you."

A Request in South Africa

Sometimes expectations of those who love us are a bit beyond our capacity. Years ago, before a temple was completed in South Africa, the Saints there who wanted to visit a temple had to travel the long and costly route to London, England, or later, to São Paulo, Brazil. When I visited South Africa they, with all the strength of their hearts and souls, petitioned me to importune President Spencer W. Kimball to seek the heavenly inspiration to erect a temple in their country. I assured them this was a matter for the Lord and His prophet. They responded, "We have faith in you, Brother Monson. Please help us."

Upon returning to Salt Lake City, I discovered that a proposed temple for South Africa had already been approved and was to be announced immediately. When this occurred, I received a telegram from our members in South Africa. It read, "Thank you, Elder Monson. We knew you could do it!" You know, I believe I never did convince them that though I approved the proposal, I did not bring it about.

Handbook for the
German Democratic Republic

§a

A great problem confronting the Church in the German Democratic Republic was to get written material to the branches and districts. I had just completed an assignment pertaining to a revision of the *General Handbook of Instructions*—a slow, detailed, three-year process.

While in the temple one Thursday morning, I said to Elder Spencer W. Kimball, "With all my heart I wish we had one copy of the German edition of the new *General Handbook of Instructions* available in the German Democratic Republic."

Brother Kimball said, "Why can't you mail one?"

I replied, "The borders are closed. Literature is *verboten*. There is no way."

Then he said, "I have another idea, Brother Monson. Why don't you, since you've worked with the *General Handbook of Instructions,* memorize it, and then we'll put you across the border?"

I laughed, and then I looked at him. He was serious.

I began the difficult assignment of attempting to memorize the *General Handbook of Instructions*. I did not commit it to memory, but I pretty well had the paragraphs, the chapters and the pages, with their contents, stored away in my mind. When I crossed the border to East Berlin, I said to our leader there, "Give me a typewriter and a ream of paper and let me work." I sat down at a table in the branch office and began to type the handbook. I was about thirty pages into it when I took time to stand. As I looked around the room, I noticed on a shelf what appeared to be the

General Handbook. I retrieved the volume and discovered that it was, indeed, the new *General Handbook,* printed in the German language. Someone had brought it across the border. I felt that all my efforts had been in vain. But for the next few years, until we updated it, I was pretty well an authority on the *General Handbook of Instructions.*

"Which One Are You?"

֍

Once when I was on assignment behind the iron curtain in Eastern Europe, I remember going to a conference where a sweet older sister came forward and asked through an interpreter, "Are you an apostle?"

When I answered, "Yes," she reached in her purse and brought forth a picture of the Quorum of the Twelve Apostles. She asked, "Which one are you?"

I looked at the picture. The junior member of the Quorum of the Twelve in that picture was John A. Widtsoe. She had not seen a member of the Twelve for a very long time! I explained that there had been a number of changes since that picture had been taken many years before.

INDEX

Index

A

Aaronic Priesthood, 10–11, 31, 36, 46, 188, 215–16
Adams, Hyrum, 61–62
Agnew family, 141–42
Allen, Howard, 125
Amputation, man who faced, 100
Airplane, woman reading Church book on, 166–68
Ambitions of author as child, 249
Angels, ministering of, 194
Apostles, picture of, in Eastern Europe, 267
Apostleship, author's call to, 259
Arbor Ward, home teaching in, 257
Archives in Swedish church, 163–64
Articles of Faith, girl who recited, 131–32
Asay, Carlos E., 241
Aspen Grove, 169

B

Baptism: performed by stutterer, 19–20; young girl who wanted, 91
Ballard, M. Russell, 92
Balmforth, Sister, 188
Bangerter, W. Grant, 181
Barber, faithful, in Canada, 227–28
Baseballs, lesson learned from, 217–18
Basketball game, author's mistake in, 252

Basketball star, honesty of, 231
Beal, Burns, 81
Ben and Emily, inactive elderly couple, 23–24
Benson, Ezra Taft, 88
Berndt, Dieter, 175–76
Bird, Margaret, 32
Bishop responsible for bringing back inactives, 59–60
Bishopric, member of, who was working on master's degree, 230
Blessings given to: women in hospital, 37–38; man in wheelchair, 47–48; man dying of cancer, 61–62; sailor on ship, 67–68; mother of missionary, 81–82; Christal, girl who had cancer, 87–90; teenage boy, who recovered, 92; child in hotel room, 115–16; badly scarred missionary, 125–26; deaf man in Australia, 155–56; blind man who sang, 223–24; elderly woman, by author and son, 225. *See also* Patriarch; Prayer
Blind man who sang, 223–24
Boy Scouts of America, conference of, 115
Boat, paper, 39–40
Book of Mormon, 113, 207
Boone, James R., 237–38
Bountiful Stake, 203
Bowring, Benjamin, 107
Branch president, calling of, 41
Brooks, Harry, 260